MENTIONS FOR *PURSUE* GOD

Frank Damazio ❘ Lead Pastor, City Bible Church

Pastor Poncho has been part of our leadership team for more than 10 years, impacting hundreds of youth and young adults. His passion to motivate youth to have a strong prayer and devotion life has resulted in the Pursue Journal and now this book, *Pursue God*. This is a great read for youth and a great tool for youth leaders. It will inspire you and arouse your passion to pursue God.

www.citybiblechurch.org

Comment On This · Love This · Share with PursueGod Community

Russell Evans ❘ Founder and Director, Planetshakers City Church

Poncho Lowder is a leader of an emerging generation. His leadership and insights are both powerful and life changing. *Pursue God* will empower and equip you to be a person who is a world changer. It is not only an essential read but also a tool to help you to build a closer relationship with God.

www.planetshakers.com

Comment On This · Love This · Share with PursueGod Community

Pastor Jude Fouquier ❘ Lead Pastor, The City Church, Ventura

Pursue God is an invitation to respond to grace and live a radically fulfilling life in relationship with God. This message is a timely word for a generation desperately seeking vision and direction. This book can serve as an effective coaching tool to help you develop daily disciplines based in authentic relationship with God that will propel you into your destiny.

Twitter: pastorjude

Comment On This · Love This · Share with PursueGod Community

Pastor Marc Estes ❘ Executive Pastor, City Bible Church

Pursue God delivers a message that is desperately needed today. There are millions who understand the value of prayer and reading the Bible but simply don't activate these critical elements in their lives. Poncho Lowder articulates the reasons why these two components are so crucial to our fruitfulness, and he delivers some incredible yet practical insights as to how to turn our inspiration into a daily reality. If you aren't willing to be completely changed, then don't read this book!

www.citybiblechurch.org

Comment On This · Love This · Share with PursueGod Community

Brandon Crouch ❘ TBN and JCTV Servant

What can anyone say about Poncho Lowder? He is pointing this generation to Jesus! I am honored to serve alongside him. *Pursue God* will change the way you do your daily devotions. It is hard-hitting and insightful and will leave the lasting impression of who Jesus is in your life!

@brandoncrouch

Comment On This · Love This · Share with PursueGod Community

Banning Liebscher | Jesus Culture Band

A generation is emerging who will be marked for Jesus not just during their you but also their entire lives. Their cry is for a fire to be ignited in their hearts that not only sustained but increases. Poncho Lowder has tackled an issue that is cr ical if we are to see this generation sustain and increase in their passion for Jesu *Pursue God* will equip you to give yourself to Jesus and His cause for your entire li This book is not an unreachable theory but an inspirational journey into practic applications that ignite long-term devotion to Jesus.

www.jesusculture.com

Comment On This · Love This · Share with PursueGod Community

Benny Perez | Lead Pastor, The Church at South Las Vegas

Poncho Lowder has given us not just the desire to pursue God but also the too to do it. I believe that every young person will benefit in his or her walk with Go by reading this book. It is a must-read for the present generation.

www.thechurchlv.com

Comment On This · Love This · Share with PursueGod Community

Elijah Waters | Worship Pastor, The City Church

Poncho Lowder has been graced with a remarkable leadership gift, and I a thrilled that God inspired him to write this book. *Pursue God* is a MUST for eve Christian, whether you are brand new in your faith or have been following Jesus f years. This book will motivate you to go deeper in your relationship with Jesus a guide you with practical steps needed for your devotional life.

www.thecity.org

Comment On This · Love This · Share with PursueGod Community

Cody Williams | Pastor and Director, Access Generation Ministri

Pursue God is exactly what this generation needs when it comes to developing deeper relationship with God and a strong devotional life! Pastor Poncho offers sights that are not only easy to understand and apply but also crucial for us to still to the next generation. Every youth pastor and leader should read this boo

Twitter: @_CodyW

Comment On This · Love This · Share with PursueGod Community

Pastor Ben Windle | Life Place Church, Brisbane, Australia

There is no doubt that a relationship with God is the most important theme of li That's why I'm so passionate about this resource! I have had the privilege working alongside Pastor Poncho in ministry, and I have seen firsthand his hea for God and his love for people. *Pursue God* is the kind of resource you will want get in the hands of as many people as possible. You'll see amazing things happer

Twitter: @benwindle

Comment On This · Love This · Share with PursueGod Community

This book is dedicated first to my family: my wife, Lora;
our three children, Hailey, Ezra and Maddie; and my parents,
Joe and Susie. Second, this book is dedicated to the key pastors
who have imparted faith and wisdom to me over the years: Frank,
Ken, Marc, Jack, Steve, Randy, Rich, Doug and Jude.

PURSUE GOD

A DISCIPLESHIP RESOURCE FROM
PONCHO LOWDER
@PASTORPONCHO

Regal

From Gospel Light
Ventura, California, U.S.A.

Published by Regal
From Gospel Light
Ventura, California, U.S.A.
www.regalbooks.com
Printed in the U.S.A.

Library of Congress Cataloging-in-Publication Data
Lowder, Poncho.
Pursue god : responding to grace / Poncho Lowder.
p. cm.
ISBN 978-0-8307-6180-7 (trade paper)
1. Spiritual life—Christianity. 2. Bible—Hermeneutics. I. Title. II. Title: Pursue
God.
BV4501.3.L695 2011
248—dc23
2011022235

Rights for publishing this book outside the U.S.A. or in non-English languages are
administered by Gospel Light Worldwide, an international not-for-profit ministry.
For additional information, please visit www.glww.org, email info@glww.org, or
write to Gospel Light Worldwide, 1957 Eastman Avenue, Ventura, CA 93003, U.S.A.

To order copies of this book and other Regal products in bulk quantities,
please contact us at 1-800-446-7735.

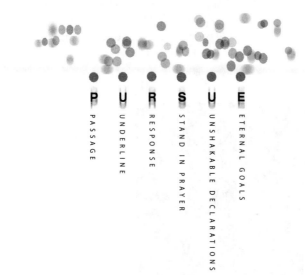

P PASSAGE

U UNDERLINE

R RESPONSE

S STAND IN PRAYER

U UNSHAKABLE DECLARATIONS

E ETERNAL GOALS

PURSUE JOURNAL
By Poncho Lowder

A perfect companion piece to the *Pursue God* book. Everyone can have a better relationship with God, and most desire just that. However, the biggest obstacle to pursuing God daily, is the daily part. A perfect companion to *Pursue God*, the book, the Pursue Journal empowers readers with the motivation and resources to have a thriving personal relationship with God. It is what readers use to implement the PURSUE devotional approach, helping them stay on track with the Bible reading plan, prayer card and journal pages. The Pursue Journal will help youth and young adults develop a thriving devotional life where they are inspired to PURSUE God daily.

ISBN: 978-0-8307-6182-1

JOIN THE PURSUE COMMUNITY

Check us out at www.PursueGod.com

Follow us on Twitter
Go to www.Twitter.com/PursueGod

Add us on Facebook
Go to www.Facebook.com/PursueGod

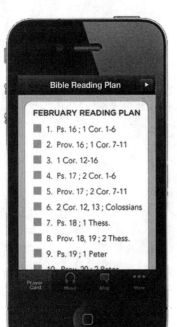

Download the
PursueGod mobile app
from
www.PursueGod.com

Contents

"REALTALK"

Cody Williams
Youth Pastor

As a pastor, I have learned that when I come to the Word in my devotions, ready to pursue my relationship with God rather than going through the motions and checking it off my spiritual "to do's" . . . He actually shows up.

Go to www.PursueGod.com to see this and other real talk quotes and interviews

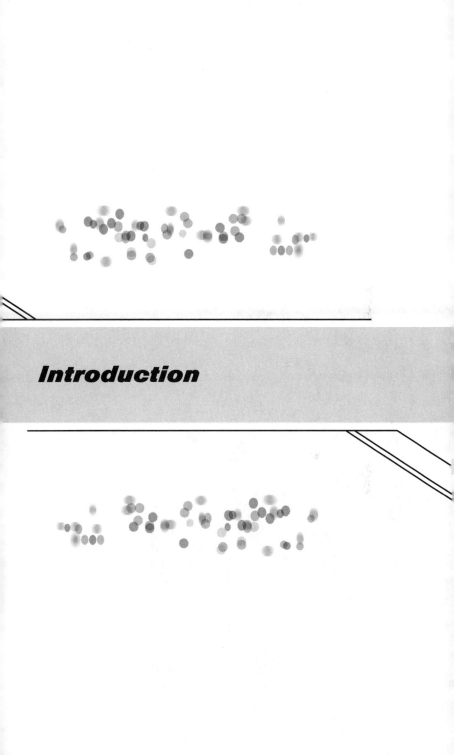

Introduction

From @PastorPoncho

God has a plan for your life that is so amazing and bigger than you could ever imagine! Take some time to listen to what He says about you.

Visit us online at www.PursueGod.com

From @PursueGod

Passion: A belief in something so real and valuable it drives you to action. Passion without action is fantasy!

More than ever, **young Christians of today are being challenged by the world around them.** With the development of social media, the technology revolution and the globalization of information on the Internet, he or she stands on the brink of a quickly developing postmodern era. There is no question that this emerging culture, with all its flashy, speedy new developments, already impacts the way in which we go about our day-to-day lives. It only makes sense that it will have an even greater impact on the way young people choose to serve God and build His church.

The way our culture communicates has changed.
Old school face-to-face isn't quite enough anymore when you live in a world where social media is the No. 1 activity on the Web. In some ways, this is great! We're more connected than ever. "Hey, I wonder what my friend five states away ate for breakfast? Maybe I'll just hop on Facebook and find out. While I'm there, I'd better let all of my acquaintances know how many hours of sleep I got last night. Also, they should really know about the dream I had while I was out. . . . Might as well post a picture of my pillow and the drool to prove it." Once, after a youth night at our church, I was pretty pumped that 23 people had made a decision for Christ. So, as I usually do when I'm excited about something, I posted on Twitter and Facebook. Amazingly, 20 minutes later, it was "Re-tweeted" by Pastor Rick Warren and made visible to 140,000 people! It's both scary and exciting to think about how many individuals worldwide can find out who you are and what you are up to.

The challenge with the effects of this shift in culture comes from the fact that the way you relate to others has a direct impact on the way you relate to God. God doesn't communicate to you the same way social media does. Sure, He cares and would love to know how you slept the night before, but that's not quite enough. He desires to have a deep and meaningful relationship with you.

Pause to examine your life with God. Is He first in your life, or just part of your life? Is He just another person on your friends list that you occasionally speak to, or is He both your Lord and Savior?

In the Bible, we see that Timothy also found himself in an emerging culture much like ours today. Immediate social connections may not have been his norm, but he *did* live in a time full of opportunity, growth and new ways of thinking. Paul, who acted as a mentor and father to Timothy, wrote his young friend two letters, found in the Bible in First and Second Timothy. Paul, who was very concerned for Timothy, wrote to encourage and challenge him to look at *why* he was pursuing God and *how* He was doing it. He wanted him to be an example to all the other people around him, both Christian and non-Christian. He also didn't want culture to have a negative impact on Timothy's relationship with God and others.

To challenge Timothy to run after God, Paul wrote, in 1 Timothy 6:11-12, "But you, man of God, flee from all this, and pursue righteousness, godliness, faith, love, endurance and gentleness. Fight the good fight of the faith." Later, in 2 Timothy 2:22, he pleaded with Timothy to "flee the evil desires of youth and pursue righteousness, faith, love and peace." Paul knew that if Timothy would focus on pursuing his heavenly Father with all of his heart, mind and strength, he would fulfill all that God had for him.

More than this, he also understood that Timothy's motives were just as important as his actions. In 2 Timothy 1:9, he asked that Timothy would pursue God and grasp God's will for his life, which is given "not according to our works, but according to His own purpose and grace" (*NASB*). Paul believed that this "grace" needed to be Timothy's No. 1 motivation if he was going to walk in God's perfect plan for his life.

It's the same for you today! **In spite of all the changes going on around you, all the craziness of the culture you live in and the busyness of your life, you will fulfill all that God has for you if you understand this grace and make a decision to pursue the One who gives it.** Take the advice of Paul and chase after God. Make Him the center of your life, not just another friend on your list! As you do, you will discover that God has great plans for you!

Much like Paul's letters to Timothy, the goal of this book is to get *you* to look at "how" you relate to God, while asking the question "why?" Why do you relate to Him the way you do? The two questions are directly related, and you can't answer one without the other. In other words, the motive for your desire to pursue God is just as important as the way you choose to pursue Him.

Remember, only God knows your real motives, and they do matter to Him. As you read through this book, let it challenge you to go deep in your relationship with God. Make it your goal to have an authentic and passionate connection with Him that doesn't resemble the shallow relationships often made in our world today. Make a daily practice of pursuing God through reading His Word and praying! Let your faith be stirred to believe that God's Word is true, and that He has great things in store for those who diligently seek Him.

PART ONE

WHY Do You PURSUE God?

Today Is the First Day of the Rest of Your Life!

Let the journey begin! I hope you are crazy excited to develop a greater relationship with God. Today, we will begin this journey together by talking about *why you pursue God.* Now, you might be thinking, *Is this going to be a book of religious duties I need to perform to be more spiritual?* The answer is no! This book is not about being religious. It's about having the best possible relationship with God.

My father once told me, **"If you want to get the full impact of doing something, you need to do it with the right understanding and the right motives."** Pursuing God is not a religious works doctrine or a means of earning grace; it's a calling all followers of Jesus have. It is an act of obedience and a response to His work of grace. You are called to seek—or pursue—God first! It's not just a good idea; it's a God idea! He desires for you to pursue Him:

> But seek first his kingdom and his righteousness, and all these things will be given to you as well (Matthew 6:33).

Throughout the Gospels, Jesus often talked to people about *why* they did something, not just *how* they did it. In Matthew 15:8-9, Jesus, quoting Isaiah, said, "These people honor me with their lips, but their hearts are far from me. They worship me in vain; their teachings are but rules taught by men." He was frustrated with them based on "why" they were doing things. **Why you do something is a big deal to God.**

So, why do you want to pursue God? Is it so you can look like a good Christian, impress a friend or feel good about yourself? Take a moment and make sure that the reason you are reading this book is not so you can climb the spiritual status ladder. Rather, it should be for the simple reason that you want a better personal relationship with God. You want to develop a deeper personal connection with Him.

Let me take you back in time for a moment. Remember when you were younger and playing hide-and-seek was the coolest game on planet Earth to play in the summer? When I was 10, I used to be one of the best players at hide-and-seek. My goal was always to be the last one found. I remember one time hiding in the ventilation system at my church and never being found until everyone gave up. I was so proud of myself! I was one of the best hiders in the whole world!

These days, I often play hide-and-seek with my kids. My four-year-old daughter, Hailey, loves for me to hide and then come and find me. As a dad, I love being found by her—she gets so excited, and it brings me great joy. I hide in the easiest places possible so she can find me quickly. Often I will hide on the couch with my feet hanging out where she can see them. I could never imagine hiding where she couldn't find me.

This is just as it is with God. God loves you so much, and He longs for you to find Him daily. He is not a "hider," and He does not take pride in being unreachable. Nor is He is a distant God who has left you here on earth to figure things out on your own. He is a loving, compassionate and faithful God who longs to be found by you. He wants you to find His will and plan for your life.

Now, while God does not hide these things from you, you *do* have to pursue Him to find them. In Jeremiah 29:11-14, God says, "I know the plans I have for you . . . plans to prosper you and not to harm you, plans to give you hope and a future. Then you will call upon me and come and pray to me, and I will listen to you. *You will seek me and find me when you seek me with all your heart. I will be found by you*" (emphasis added).

As you read this book, you are going to be inspired to pursue God more than ever before. When you take time to pursue God each day, you will grow closer to Him. The reality of who He is and the calling He has on your life will become more and more evident. So be encouraged—God wants to have a deep and meaningful relationship with you. As you pursue Him, you can expect Him to bless you. As the author of Hebrews states:

> But without faith it is impossible to please Him, for he who comes to God must believe that He is, and that He is a rewarder of those who diligently seek Him (Hebrews 11:6, *NKJV*).

Remember that you are not in this pursuit alone. We are all on a journey of pursuing God. So, to help and encourage you along the way, throughout the book there are "Real Talk" pages that have testimonies of real people and their journey of pursuing God. These stories are inspiring and will challenge you in your pursuit. You can go to **www.PursueGod.com** to watch their entire interview and see many others.

Well, buckle your seat belt and get ready to pursue God like never before!

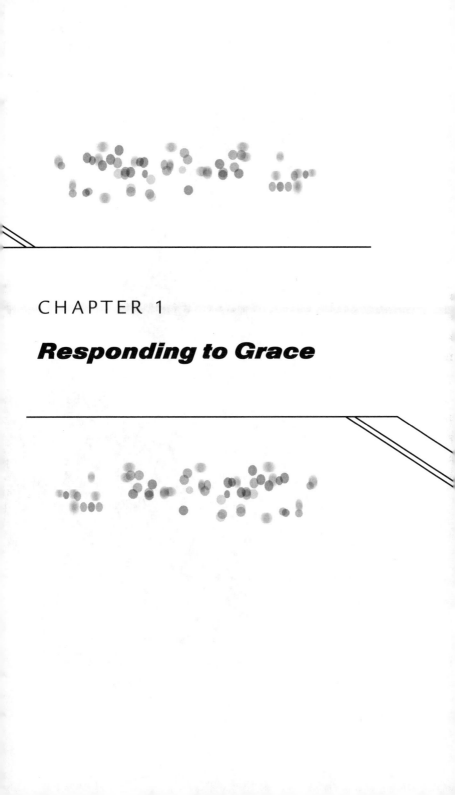

CHAPTER 1

Responding to Grace

"Why should I pursue God?" a young man asked me with a deep sense of frustration in his voice. *Very good question,* **I thought and was about to answer when I was silenced by the shouts of an angry coffee drinker.** Apparently, his latte didn't meet the high standards of a Pacific Northwesterner. As any pastor in Portland who *needs* his Stumptown coffee must learn to do, I tuned the coffee crazy out and continued our conversation.

From our time together, I gathered that **he, like so many others his age, wanted to know God's will for his life** but didn't want to put the extra effort into finding it. Often, young people have a desire for knowledge but no passion for the journey. They would rather just text Google and get the immediate information they're used to getting. Unfortunately, God doesn't respond to a click or a text. He responds to a relationship; and strong, meaningful relationships take time and effort.

As I sat facing this young man in the noisy coffee shop, my mind began to wander. I thought of all I could say in response to his question . . .

Before the earth was ever created, God made a decision that He wanted to have a relationship with you. He knew this relationship would not be easy or without a price. As He created the heavens and the earth, and all the living things, He did it with one thing in mind . . . *you*! You are the only part of His creation that was made in His image and has eternal relational capability.

Before you ever chose God, He made a decision to pursue you at any expense! Just open your Bible to page one and read. Adam and Eve were created and placed in a Garden that contained everything they would ever need. God loved them so much that He created this place where they could be together forever.

Yet, it was in the middle of this Garden that they chose to walk away from Him. **He had so passionately pursued a relationship, and *this* was their response.** Rather than revel in all that God had said and done for them, they chose to listen to the voice of a questioning, distracting serpent. This choice led them to sin and separation. *They were soon lost in the Garden that He had created just for them.*

How do you get lost when you are in the place that God specifically made for you? As Adam and Eve found, sin will do the trick. Sin changes the way you see yourself and the people around you. It blurs your vision and hinders you from moving forward in life.

What's truly amazing is that after they committed this sin, God immediately pursued them. "Adam, where are you?" He asked, His majestic voice filling the whole Garden. It was not as though the all-powerful Creator of the world didn't know where Adam and Eve were. He simply wanted them to know that in spite of their sin, He was still going to seek after them. He still wanted relationship. They were right in the center of where God wanted them to be; yet, they had found themselves lost. Lucky for them, God's love outweighed even their greatest sin and inability to obey His one commandment.

I often think, *Why did they do it? Why did they listen to a serpent? Couldn't they just be content with all they had? I would never talk to a snake. Who does that?! Really, Adam and Eve? Really?!* It's easy to point the finger and play the "really?" game with our great-great-great . . . grandparents. But if we examine the world around us today, we'll find things are no different! **God has given us all a free will, and all mankind has made a decision to sin.** The good news is that God is also the same today. He loves you and is willing to pursue you in spite of all the bad you have done. The Bible says, "While we were still sinners, Christ died for us" (Romans 5:8). The result of sin is that it separates you from God. This is a problem that could only be fixed by Christ. To pursue you, He sacrificed His life. He desired so greatly to have a relationship with you that He paid the ultimate price to get that chance! This is the greatest act of grace! As C. S. Lewis put it, "He died not for men, but for each man. If each man had been the only man made, He would have done no less." Knowing that you would possibly reject His gift of grace and forgiveness, He still went to that cross and died for you.

So, a lot of thoughts were running through my head as I sat in the loud coffeehouse café. The crazy guy had finally calmed down, and I was ready with my answer to the question, "Why should I pursue God?" I looked at the young man in front of me and said, **"Out of a response to His grace. You should pursue God because, well, God first pursued you!** Not that you could earn or pay back His gift of grace. That's impossible! But, you *get* to respond to it! If you want to have a relationship that is more than a Sunday experience, then you need to daily pursue Him!" Okay, so not your average coffee-talk; but when you get a revelation, you've got to preach.

Many people are just like this young man, lacking direction and unable to grasp God's will for their lives. Yet, like him,

"*REALTALK*"

Cris Buck

I pursue God daily because I know I need His grace. When I'm weak, He strengthens me. When my perspective is wrong, He renews my mind. When I stand in His presence, I am made whole. This grace is the extension of his love. It causes me to pursue Him.

Go to www.PursueGod.com to see this and other real talk quotes and interviews

they have not made a decision to pursue a deeper relationship with their Creator. "Submit yourselves, then, to God," it says in James 4:7-8; "Resist the devil, and he will flee from you. Come near to God and he will come near to you." It's that simple! If you respond to His grace and pursue God, you will find yourself closer to Him than ever! In Jeremiah 29:13-14, God says it this way: "You will seek me and find me when you seek me with all your heart. I will be found by you." When you make a decision to respond to God's grace and pursue Him, the Bible makes it clear that the result will be a dynamic relationship with Him.

It's important that you don't do this seeking out of a works mentality—that you don't do it to earn His favor. If this is a hard concept to grasp, just imagine if someone bought you a brand-new car, your dream car! He showed up at your house, handed you the keys and claimed he just wanted to bless you with it. No one would deny that this scenario is pretty awesome. But let's imagine further . . . What if you responded by saying, "Hey, I'll give you $10 to help pay for it. That'll cover part of it at least!" We can all agree this is a lame attempt at paying back an incredible gift.

Just as your $10 bill won't do the trick, you can't pay God back for His act of grace in your life with your works. But you *can* respond to it! He gave His only son to pay the price for your sin. You could never pay this back, and He doesn't expect you to. He simply wants you to accept it and live a life in response to it!

In these next several chapters, as we delve into the "Why?" and "How?" of pursuing God, you will be challenged to take a fresh look at the way you are responding to God's gift of grace. Is your response a "have to" or a "get to"? Do you find yourself motivated to take time to chase after God daily as a response to His grace? Or, do you act out the motions of Christianity with a "works" mentality? Challenge yourself to go deeper in your relationship with God through daily devotions—reading His Word and praying. Use the Pursue Journal or any means necessary to latch on to your Creator and go deeper in your relationship with Him.

Don't be like Adam and Eve, lost in the place and the calling that God had created *just* for them. Understand all that God has done for you by His grace, respond to it and be prepared to draw closer to Him and live a life full of purpose.

"REALTALK"

Sami Logan
(Quote from Video interview)

I didn't know where to start in the Bible—it was a huge book! It was really good to have a plan that broke it down daily for me . . .

Go to www.PursueGod.com to see this and other real talk quotes and interviews

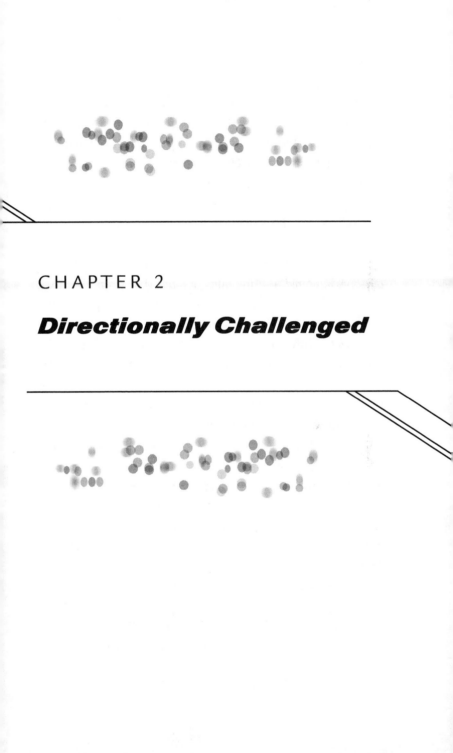

CHAPTER 2

Directionally Challenged

"Where should I go to college?" Lisa asked, with a look of absolute confusion on her face. So many choices were laid out before her. "Should I spend $1,300 a year or $32,000 a year on college? What should I major in? Once I nail that down, which school has the best opportunities for that major? Should I stay local? Or would moving far away be good for me? What if I end up changing my mind while I'm there?"

This is where I'm supposed to wave the old magic wand and tell her *exactly* where God wants her to go. Easy, right? Wrong. Sometimes, I feel like young people think I'm the Bible Answer Man: *Buy him a cup of coffee and get all your tough questions answered!* But in reality, it's not that simple.

Lisa, like so many others before her, was hoping that I had a map for her life. She needed to know what the next few turns were. Unfortunately, I couldn't tell her that. Even if I *did* hold that map, I would most likely just get the poor girl lost.

As my wife puts it, I'm "directionally challenged." She says I have a special ability when driving to get as far from the intended location in the shortest amount of time possible. Personally, I feel that's stretching it a little. I like to think my divine male instinct guides me. Sadly, that instinct doesn't always get me to where I'm supposed to be.

A week before I sat down to write this, I was outside the San Francisco Bay area with three of the pastors from my church, City Bible, in Portland, Oregon. As usual, we found ourselves extremely lost in the Oakland Hills. There we were with our Internet maps in hand, thinking, *This should be a breeze.* Unfortunately, for a map to be of any use, you have to know where you are on that map! We had no clue. There is nothing worse than four directionally challenged

"REALTALK"

Matt Bushard
Youth Pastor

As a pastor and worship leader, having daily devotions is key! It's so important to be connected to God as our source for everything. The Bible comes alive and real when you consistently spend time reading it and letting it impact and change your life. Daily devotions are key to unlocking the destiny God has for you!

Go to www.PursueGod.com to see this and other real talk quotes and interviews

guys driving around convinced that they know the way. Living in total denial, we each took turns getting the group more and more lost. After about 40 minutes of driving in circles, an idea finally popped into my head. I knew the church was north of our current location, so I decided to just drive north until we hit the freeway. Using the little compass on the rental car, we found the I-580. From there, it was smooth sailing!

During the last 13 years of being in and around youth ministry, I've found that the pursuit of God works very similarly. **If you try to use the Bible and your relationship with God to map everything out, rather than use them as a compass, you tend to get lost. Life can throw you a curve ball and suddenly you're stuck driving in circles with no real clarity.** How do you figure out the next step when you're in a different place than you thought you'd be? Where are you on the map you've made for yourself?

Maps are great if you constantly know where you are and where you're going. But that's not the case for most people. You might have a *sense* of the direction God wants you to go, but no one has the *entire* map figured out.

As I found in our little Oakland adventure, a compass can often be more useful than a map. In the same way, rather than looking for a specific grid with every step laid out, you need to let the Word of God and your relationship with Him act as a compass for you! If you know how to use it properly, a compass can be a very powerful, dependable tool. Regardless of the circumstances, its needle *always* points north. You can count on it. It is not designed to tell you exactly where you are, but it still guides you along the way. God's Word works the same way. It's not meant to be a mile marker. It's meant to be a light unto your path!

Lisa sat across from me in my office, awaiting the big answers to her college plans. Finally, I decided to just say it. **"You're directionally challenged,"** I told her, and she gave me a funny look. So, I continued . . . "You are constantly looking for a map from God and not finding it. You're overwhelmed with all of life's choices. You don't know what to do regarding college because you don't know how to pursue God. If you were pursuing God regularly, His will would be clear to you. It's not like He's trying to hide it. I know you desire the next step, but His Word is not meant to be something you casually glance at to get direction. Rather, it should be an internal compass, constantly pointing you toward where He wants you."

Lisa just stared at the disco ball in my office with a confused look on her face. I could tell that she wasn't fully getting what I was saying, so I decided to take a few minutes to talk about the life of Joseph. He definitely had a compass mentality. As you read in Genesis 37, things start out well for him when he gets a great word spoken over his life through a dream. It seems as though he's heading toward a great life, until it all falls apart on him. His brothers throw him in a pit and then sell him off into slavery! Big bummer.

Now, if he'd had a map mentality, he would have been very lost at this point in his life and probably just gotten mad at God and given up. But our pal Joe didn't take that route. Instead, he just kept moving north, making the best of every situation. From the pit to the palace to the prison, Joseph kept trusting in God and seeking after Him. It was only after many hard years that we finally see Joseph get to the place he felt God had been calling him to.

It was in this final, triumphant season that he made one of the most profound statements of his life to his brothers: "But Joseph said to them, 'Don't be afraid. Am I in the place of God? You intended to harm me, but God intended it for good to accomplish what is now being done, the saving of many lives'" (Genesis 50:19-20). **What an amazing perspective! Joseph was not spending his life looking for the map; he simply lived life with a compass that was focused on God's will, knowing that it would lead him in the right direction.** Ultimately, he was in the exact place God destined him to be, and an entire nation was saved from devastation because of it.

My conversation with Lisa continued for a while as we shifted from Joseph's to Lisa's relationship with God. It turned out that she didn't have much of a devotional life at all. When she *did* read her Bible and pray, it was in an effort to get some kind of immediate direction from God. She had a spiritual map mentality when she needed a consistent compass mentality. Together, we looked at her daily schedule and found a good 30-minute window in her morning routines that she could set aside. She was ready to use this time to chase after God through praying, reading and journaling in her Pursue Journal.

If you were to talk to Lisa today, she would tell you that she now seeks God daily with the goal of going deep in her relationship with Him. She knows that when the big questions come, the compass in her heart will give her a strong sense of God's direction.

What about you? Do you approach your time with God using a map mentality or a compass mentality? Take a moment today and put in your daily schedule time to pursue God. Make it a priority in your life! Helen Keller once said, "To be blind is a terrible thing, but what is worse is that there are people who can see but have no vision for their life." Vision comes from the compass in your heart that leads you toward God's destination. PURSUE God; let Him reveal the right direction and you'll find true vision.

Flee the evil desires of youth and pursue righteousness, faith, love and peace, along with those who call on the Lord out of a pure heart.
2 TIMOTHY 2:22

Vision comes from the compass in your heart that leads you toward God's destination. PURSUE God; **let Him reveal the right direction** and you'll find true vision.

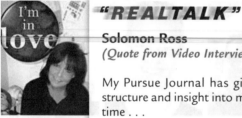

"*REALTALK*"

~~Solomon Ross~~
(Quote from Video Interview)

My Pursue Journal has given me new structure and insight into my devotional time . . .

Go to www.PursueGod.com to see this and other real talk quotes and interviews

CHAPTER 3

It's Time to Run

There is nothing quite like sitting down on your couch after a long, crazy day and watching sports finals—baseball, football, soccer, basketball, the Olympics, even golf! I don't care about all these sports so much as I enjoy getting caught up in the intensity of people pursuing their dreams. I'm always amazed at the look in their eyes as they draw near to all they have given their life to. My favorite is finals time, where it's all on the line. If you lose, you're out of the running for that season. **I've seen grown men cry; petite women yell with the rage of a sumo wrestler; and many push their bodies beyond belief as they get within reach of their dream.**

During the winter Olympics of 2010, one of my favorite speed skaters, Apolo Anton Ohno, was racing in the 1,500-meter race. Everyone knew that he had a good chance to win a medal, but nothing was guaranteed. He had trained for years, this was his third Olympics, and he was possibly going to break the USA record for the most medals by a speed skater. Needless to say, the pressure was high. Just watching from my couch, it was impossible to miss the focus and intensity on his face. Apolo was there to win.

As he pulled up to the starting line, he took a big yawn like always and then looked straight down the track. The gun went off, and he calmly started at the back of the pack. For a guy in last place, he looked very relaxed. He knew he had enough time to slowly and methodically work his way toward the front of the pack. In third place, coming into the final lap, he really turned things up. Flying around the turn, Apolo swung wide, picked up some speed, and passed everyone to take the gold medal. How amazing it was to see him explode on that final lap as he pursued his dream of gold!

You need to live life in much the same way—with it all on the line, holding back nothing, going for the gold. Don't look back all the time at your past mistakes and weaknesses; look forward with complete passion and intensity. Now is the time to give all your mind, heart and strength to going after God and what He has called you to do. You only get one lifetime to pursue Him. Make it count.

It's Time to Run!

How are you living your life? Are you consumed with a constant desire to pursue all that God has for you? To pursue means to "passionately seek after something or someone." This is what you've been called to do: not to simply walk toward Him, but to run after Him with everything you have, to seek Him with grand expectation! You've been told time and time again that life is a race; but have you ever thought about the finish line?

You have been called to pursue the destiny of God. It's the gold medal waiting for you if you chase after it. As you run this race, your relationship with God is not limited to a simple salvation experience. That's just the starting line. Once you take off, your purpose will be fulfilled if you pursue God. Paul says in 1 Corinthians 9:24-27:

> Do you not know that in a race all the runners run, but only one gets the prize? Run in such a way as to get the prize. Everyone who competes in the games goes into strict training. They do it to get a crown that

"*REALTALK*"

Nikki Dasso
College Student

I hold prayer and the Word of God responsible for every positive life change that I have been through. Not one time have I sat down to pray or to read the Word and regretted it—God always speaks, always encourages, and always strengthens me!

Go to www.PursueGod.com to see this and other real talk quotes and interviews

will not last; but we do it to get a crown that will last forever. Therefore I do not run like a man running aimlessly; I do not fight like a man beating the air. No, I beat my body and make it my slave so that after I have preached to others, I myself will not be disqualified for the prize.

It's easy to get distracted from the finish line when you don't know what you're pursuing. You need to know what and why you're pursuing something. In Zig Ziglar's book *Over the Top*, the author illustrates this notion beautifully:

At the Summer Olympic Games in Mexico City in 1968, a runner named John Stephen Aquara ran in the marathon, representing Tanzania. Shortly after the race began, Aquara fell, causing serious injuries to both a knee and an ankle. He received some medical attention and then, bandaged and still bleeding, got back on the trail and resumed the race. He limped, hobbled, and skipped. Two hours after the other competitors had finished, John Stephen Aquara crossed the finish line. He even took a victory lap around the stadium. When a reporter later asked him why he had continued in the race when it was clear he could win no medal, Aquara replied, "My country didn't send me seven thousand miles to enter the race. They sent me here to finish the race."[1]

Can you imagine watching that guy limp across the finish line, seeing the determination in his face? He knew exactly what he was there for. Tragedy struck, just like it always seems to do, but

Aquara didn't quit. It wasn't enough for him just to be in the race; he wanted to finish. And, it wasn't enough just to finish; he did so as strong as he possibly could.

All right, I could talk sports all day, but it's time for the deep questions: Why are you living your life the way you are? Why are you pursuing the things you are pursuing? Are you content just being a Christian by title? Does simply going to church each week satisfy your religious quota? God has called you to do more than just sit on the starting line of salvation. He is calling you to passionately pursue Him and live your life with purpose!

What is your motive for running the race of life? For pursuing God? You shouldn't try to earn God's favor or appease His anger. You shouldn't run the race hoping your "works" will win it for you. You should pursue God out of a response to His grace and with a desire to know Him more and get closer to Him!

Paul reminds us in Romans 9:30-32 that "the Gentiles, who did not pursue righteousness, have obtained it, a righteousness that is by faith; but Israel, who pursued a law of righteousness, has not attained it. Why not? Because they pursued it not by faith but as if it were by works. They stumbled over the 'stumbling stone.' " Make sure you keep your relationship with God a passionate journey of faith, not a work to repay Him for what He did for you. Run the race with the determination of an Olympic athlete who knows inside and out what he/she wants. Let the desire to "win," or to walk in God's amazing destiny, beat in your veins as you chase after the finish line.

Note

1. Zig Ziglar, *Over the Top* (Nashville, TN: Thomas Nelson, 1997), n.p.

"REALTALK"

~~Jared Donald~~
Young Adults Leader

I learned the importance of pursuing God as a youth, and looking back I see how vital it was for me to daily experience an authentic relationship with God.

Go to www.PursueGod.com to see this and other real talk quotes and interviews

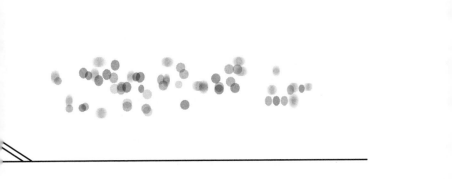

CHAPTER 4

The Passionate Pursuit

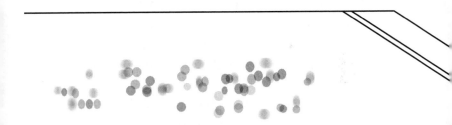

A belief in something so real and valuable that it drives you to action. **This is the true meaning of passion.** But it is more than just a thought. Biblical passion must have an action attached to it! It also must have a goal that is "real and valuable." Today, people pursue personal success, seeking greatness, money, fame, happiness, and so on. In a country where you can always obtain more, be more and accomplish more, material success has become the focal point of daily life. Who can get rich the youngest? Who can obtain fame and fortune by age 22? By age 17? By age 12? Whether it's through pursuing entertainment careers or working hard to get into the top schools, young people are constantly measured by how early they can be deemed "financially successful."

The problem with this way of thinking comes from the fact that you can have worldly success in life without having true significance! God has called you to pursue a life that means something. Don't live aimlessly, going after the shallow things of this world. Instead, live life passionately for God.

I have found that it is often this passion that takes people from average to extraordinary. Recently, I was riding back from a worship night in Seattle, Washington, with my friend Yas. Today, Yas is an amazing guitarist in the Generation Unleashed Band. During our three-hour journey back to Portland, I seized the opportunity to find out more about his story.

Yas grew up in Japan with a loving father who put in a lot of hours at work. Yas was not a Christian, but he had a

Christian friend who took him to church every once in a while. As a boy, he learned to play the piano, but that was short-lived. It wasn't until he was 15 that he picked up a guitar. During his teenage years, he would practice every day for at least an hour, and slowly found himself getting better and better.

When he was 17, Yas went to a youth camp. There, after a powerful worship service where he experienced the presence of God, he made the decision to become a follower of Jesus Christ. Up to that point, Yas described himself as just an "okay" guitarist. It wasn't until the next few years that he discovered he actually possessed an amazing gift.

After a short amount of time, he was playing in the church band and began to develop a strong passion for the unique presence of God he experienced when playing the guitar. He found himself practicing three to five hours a day! He explained to me that as he grew closer to God, his passion overtook him and became the sole focus of his life.

Today, I would describe Yas as a world-class guitarist, and definitely the best I know. While we were driving back to Portland together, I asked him, "What do you think was the key to your becoming so good at playing the guitar?" He answered with two thoughts. First, he pointed to the passion he had developed for God and for his instrument. Second, he said he found himself able to eliminate many of the distractions that get in most other people's way.

You can learn a lot from Yas's life, passions and discipline. If you are going to achieve greatness in anything, you have to push beyond distractions. This is especially the case when it comes to your relationship with God. Today more than ever, so many things can divert you from pursuing Him: TV, sports, video games, Facebook, movies, relationships, and so on. If you really want the greatest life you can live, you must be willing to place all these distractions aside and pursue God with passion, first and foremost.

One of my favorite Scripture passages is Hebrews 12:1-2:

Let us throw off everything that hinders and the sin that so easily entangles. And let us run with perseverance the race marked out for us, fixing our eyes on Jesus, the pioneer and perfecter of faith.

In this passage, the author of Hebrews challenges us to "throw off everything that hinders" as well as "sin." In other words, running the race for God involves more than just avoiding sin. If you are going to passionately pursue God, you have to deal with the distractions and weights that hinder you. This means letting go of things you have been holding on to and looking inside your heart at your motives. From there, you must take external action to change.

Are you passionately pursuing God? Do your actions reveal a passion for Him? God designed you to live a life that pursues Him, a life of action. This means more than just reading the Bible and saying some scripted prayer. It's not simply a religious practice. It's a relational experience. But what exactly does this "experience" look like?

Over the course of my life, I've noticed five values that most passionate people possess. Everyone has areas of their life they could work on to be more passionate. As you read through these marks of a passionate person, ask yourself if they are truly activated in your life, and not just perceived to be.

Five Marks of a Passionate Pursuer

1. To *passionately pursue God, you need to have a yielded heart.* By nature, no one is given to putting others first. Each of us has a built-in drive called the "sin nature." This drive likes to yield to no one. I think of it much like my sister behind the wheel. Everyone else needs to stop so she can get where she wants to go. To have a yielded heart, you need to align your passions and desires with God's Word. Whenever your heart and His Word don't align, defer to God's way, not *your* way.

2. To *passionately pursue God, you need to have a focused mind.* It's no secret that life contains lots of potential distractions. In our fast-paced society, everything is competing for your full attention. If you're going to pursue God's will, you have to be intentional about keeping your focus. Paul says it this way, in Colossians 3:2: "Set your minds on things above, not on earthly things."

3. To *passionately pursue God, you need to have a surrendered will.* In a culture of opportunity, pressure and materialism, letting go of your agenda is easier said than done. Young people are constantly taught to seek after whatever they want, to go big and go fast. Our culture encourages each individual to put himself/herself at the

center of all decisions, rather than God. By surrendering your will and allowing God to be your leader and guide, you can avoid many of the setbacks that the enemy has planned for you. Pursuing God with a surrendered will doesn't guarantee that your life will be all "happy, happy," but it does ensure that it will be purpose-driven and significant!

4. *To passionately pursue God, you need to have a committed lifestyle.* Many people confuse desire with commitment. They have a lot of "perceived" values instead of "practiced" values. Often, these perceived values come at no expense to the lifestyle they want to live. If you are going to truly pursue God, you need to adjust your lifestyle. You need to prioritize, making time to get into the Word, to pray and to act out Christ's principles found in His Word.

5. *To passionately pursue God, you need to have a persistent attitude.* Pursuing God is not a sprint, it's a marathon. It's about making a decision to continuously go after God with everything you've got, and not deviating from it. Life is full of challenges every day that can keep you from moving forward in your pursuit of God. It takes a consistent desire, each day, that is not limited to your emotional state of being, and a persistent attitude that is willing to go after God, no matter what the day might hold.

Every dream has a price. My friend Yas had a strong dream. To attain it, he had to continually evaluate his life

"REALTALK"

Jeff Borota

There is no greater feeling in the world then waiting on the creator of the universe, the author of all salvation and receiving a word of encouragement.

Go to www.PursueGod.com to see this and other real talk quotes and interviews

and make sure he was doing all that was necessary. Take some time right now and evaluate *your* life. Be honest about how passionate you are when it comes to pursuing God. Like most things, passion is developed as you do something more and more. In his guitar playing, Yas went through ups and downs. Sometimes all he could think about was his guitar; and other times, he found himself frustrated and not that thrilled about it. Most likely, you can identify with this part of Yas's story. **Your passion level as you pursue God may not always be the strongest, and that's okay. The important thing is to be aware of what it is that you are giving your heart, mind and strength to.** Constantly evaluate your life and your walk with God so that you can stay on track even during the hard times.

"REALTALK"

Dylan Jones
Youth Pastor

Even after going through four years of Bible college, the greatest revelation I have had is how vital a personal relationship with Jesus is. That is what the Pursue Journal has helped me with . . . connection with Jesus daily.

Go to www.PursueGod.com to see this and other real talk quotes and interviews

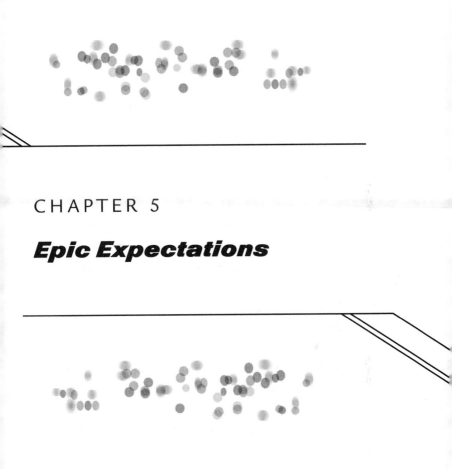

CHAPTER 5

Epic Expectations

Where do I find my hope? Who can I put my trust in?
Where do I find my peace?
It comes from you.
Where do I find my joy? What is this Love I'm feeling?
Where do I find my strength?
It comes from You.
Jesus you're everything, and I'll give my life to you,
Live my life for you . . .
All things are possible with You,
All things are possible with You[1]

These are the simple, yet powerful lyrics of one of my favorite songs, "All Things," by one of the Generation Unleashed worship leaders, Jeremy Scott. Every time I play it on my iPod or we sing it in our worship services, my faith gets stirred up. It's easy to forget that there's nothing too big for our God; the song works as a simple reminder. As it proclaims that statement—"all things are possible with You"—over and over in the bridge, it begins to sink into my mind and heart. Nothing is too great for Him! *All* things are possible when I'm in relationship with God!

All too often, people tend to limit what God can do in their lives. Fear, failure and simple lack of faith can easily keep someone from reaching out for all that God has planned for him or her. Does this sound familiar?

You need to be reminded that God wants to do *epic* things in and through you. That word "epic" refers to something that is "beyond your grasp or ability." The things that

God wants for you are far beyond what you could attain on your own. Paul describes this in 1 Corinthians 2:9, stating, "No eye has seen, no ear has heard, no mind has conceived what God has prepared for those who love Him."

God has amazing things in store for you! As you read His Word, you should be inspired to believe for those things. Never forget that God is a loving Father who gets excited about being around His children and always has something waiting for them! Draw near to your Father and expect Him to speak to you in a personal way.

This idea of expectation is so important when you've decided to engage in a passionate pursuit. The PURSUE approach, which we will delve into soon, centers around daily devotions—a practice I think works best when one comes with Epic Expectations. I've listed five of those that help me when I approach the Word each day. You should try them and see how much deeper you are able to go with the Father who so lovingly waits to spend time with you.

EPIC EXPECTATION #1
God Will Speak to You Through His Word!

We are told in Hebrews 4:12 that "the word of God is living and active. Sharper than any double-edged sword, it penetrates even to dividing soul and spirit, joints and marrow; it judges the thoughts and attitudes of the heart." How amazing that God wants to talk with you and that as you read His Word, it will speak to your heart and mind! As the Scripture describes, it's "active," meaning it's always working on us as we read it. When you sit down with your Bible each day, have an Epic Expectation that God will speak to you through His Word.

EPIC EXPECTATION #2
God Will Reveal His Plan and Will for You!

It's so cool to me that God doesn't keep His plans hidden from us. Paul says in Romans 12:1-2:

> Therefore, I urge you, brothers, in view of God's mercy, to offer your bodies as living sacrifices, holy and pleasing to God—this is your spiritual act of worship. Do not conform any longer to the pattern of this world, but be transformed by the renewing of your

"*REALTALK*"

Dustin Hutley

I couldn't be who God wants me to be without seeking Him and Him seeking me on a daily basis. His Word guides me daily, I consistently declare it over my life!

Go to www.PursueGod.com to see this and other real talk quotes and interviews

mind. Then you will be able to test and approve what God's will is—his good, pleasing and perfect will.

This passage reveals that God wants you to know what He has in store for you. It's not something He hides. You don't have to play the guessing game with God. As you read the Word and pray, He will speak to you about your destiny, your purpose and His "pleasing and perfect will" for you. Have an Epic Expectation that God will clearly reveal His will for you as you spend time with Him.

This is what the Lord says, he who made the earth, the Lord who formed it and established it—the Lord is his name: "Call to me and I will answer you and tell you great and unsearchable things you do not know."
JEREMIAH 33:2-3 (EMPHASIS ADDED)

EPIC EXPECTATION #3
Your Faith Will Grow!

In Romans 10:17, Paul says that "faith comes from hearing the message, and the message is heard through the word of Christ." A daily and consistent devotional life is key to continually growing in your faith. **Having faith will help you through the hard times of life.** Faith will also give you the confidence to stand when the enemy comes against you. Along with all this, when others are going through hard times, you will have a source of faith to draw from so that they might lean on you for strength. Have an Epic Expectation that God will grow your faith every day as you spend time in His Word!

EPIC EXPECTATION #4
You Will Get to Know God Better!

One of my personal life heroes is Kevin Conner, an amazing pastor, teacher and man of God. I will never forget a comment he made in one of the classes I took at Portland Bible College. He said, "God's Word is His will, and His will is His Word. Therefore, if you want to know God more, spend ample time in His Word!" I have never forgotten that advice. Every time I read my Bible, I expect to get to know God more. As I dive into my reading, I learn about His personality, what He likes and dislikes, how He responds in different situations, and so much more. Time in God's Word is the best way to develop a greater relationship with Him. Think of it like this: He wrote the whole Bible just so you could get to know Him and His will for your life! Have an Epic Expectation that the more you read His Word, the more you'll understand about your God.

EPIC EXPECTATION #5
You Will Receive Wisdom for the Day Ahead of You!

Every day that you read, you should expect God to give you wisdom to help guide and protect you. Believing this, David wrote in Psalm 119:105, "Your word is a lamp to my feet and a light for my path." Earlier, in Psalm 119:9-11, he asked, "How can a young man keep his way pure?" Answering his own question, he proclaimed, "By living according to Your word. I seek You with all my heart; do not let me stray from Your commands. I have hidden Your word in my heart that I might not sin against you." David had great expectation that the Word of God would give him direction and keep him on the path of purity. That is why you should also have an Epic Expectation that the wisdom you need will come when you read the Bible daily.

Today, as you discover the PURSUE approach to daily devotions, let the Generation Unleashed band's lyrics ring in your ear: *"All things are possible with You."* Remind yourself of this and be filled with expectation like David's and Paul's. Know that as you set aside time for daily devotions and approach them with Epic Expectations, **God will give you the wisdom you'll need for the day ahead of you.** He knows what you need even before you need it. He's just waiting for you to spend time with Him so that He might reveal to you that all things are possible through Him.

Once you've made a decision to do this and you begin your discovery of the limitless power of God, it's time to step into action. We've discussed *why* you pursue God; now let's move into the *how*. The next section is dedicated to teaching you the practical steps toward pursuing God and building a deep, dynamic relationship with Him. The goal of the rest of this book is to equip you with the keys to develop a strong devotional life that will weather the storms of life—the good times, the busy times, the hard times and the unexplainable times.

Note
1. Jeremy Scott, "All Things," used by permission.

PART TWO

HOW Do You PURSUE God?

Passion Without Action Is Fantasy— True Passion Will Always Have Action Attached to It

We have spent the first half of this book discussing *why* we pursue God. With this understanding that it's a response to His grace, we can move forward and spend the rest of the book talking about *how* to pursue Him more effectively. By now, I hope you understand that the motivation for daily pursuit of God is not to rack up the "works" points; it's about passion! It's not done from obligation, but from joyful anticipation of getting closer to God and spending time in His presence.

Most Christians today struggle with doing daily devotions because they have never developed a consistent approach to their Bible reading. They have allowed this act of reading God's Word to become subject to their changing emotional state each morning. Unfortunately, for most people, this equates to hitting the snooze button five times instead of waking up and opening the Good Book.

When I was younger, I, like so many others, struggled with consistency in my spiritual devotional time. I had no idea how to "do" devotions and get something out of it. Because of this, they quickly became a religious experience rather than a relational encounter. It wasn't until I was taught that there was more to devotions than just reading that I had a major breakthrough.

Today when I approach my morning devotions, I come prepared to receive from God, because I know that He wants to meet with me. He has a passion to hear from me and to speak into my life. I have a daily pattern that I follow, but the routine doesn't go stale with time. Instead, I find it allows me maximum personal growth. If you have a hard time believing this, let me tell you about three types of people and their approach to daily devotions. Which type are you?

Let's liken daily devotions to working out. Remember your last trip to the local health club? You probably found, like I did, that there are three types of people walking around that bustling center of exercise and discipline. In one corner of the gym is "The New Guy," the person who doesn't really have a clue. He's just started his gym membership, and he's eyeing the rowing machine like it's some kind of torture device. In the other corner, there's "The Know-It-All." This person knows what's up. He can tell you everything about each and every machine, how to do the hardest reps and which protein bars are optimal. He'll laugh when you make mistakes, and yet when it comes down to it, he doesn't really appear to ever use the equipment himself. Finally, there is "The Body Builder," the person you'd think twice before messing with. You see him there every day, consistent in his workouts, displaying endurance and focus. He follows a pattern, and his body obviously shows it.

Which type are you?

Lots of Christians are like the first person. They go to the Word and immediately find themselves overwhelmed. How do you use this thing? Where do you even start? Often, they walk right out of the "health club" (the routine of daily devotions). There are also a lot of Christians like the Know-It-All. They talk about the importance of reading and journaling, and they truly sound like they have it all together. Yet, they lack the seen power of God's Word acting in their lives. It may come as a shock, but only a small percent of Christians today actually live life like the third person: the "Body Builder," possessing a consistent, daily devotional life. When you meet one of these rarities who understands the importance of a Bible reading routine, you can see how the simple action is impacting their lives. Just as you can see the Body Builder's bulging muscles, when someone is passionate about his or her daily devotions, the results in their life are tangible and undeniable.

Let's Get to the Practical Stuff

As we go through this next section of the book, I plan to teach you a powerful way to approach your daily devotions. I call it "PURSUE". This acronym can help you go deeper in your devotional time by teaching you a holistic approach. Its goal is to maximize your time with God, while not boxing you into a religious experience. If after reading this book, you find that you want a Pursue Journal to help you with this approach, you can get one at www.PursueGod.com. But for now, let's lay out what these letters stand for.

"REALTALK"

Isaac Tarter
Worship Pastor

Worship and devotions go hand in hand as an essential reminder in our lives of what our right and proper response is to God. It brings us closer into alignment with His plan and purpose for us that we would be who he wants us to be.

Go to www.PursueGod.com to see this and other real talk quotes and interviews

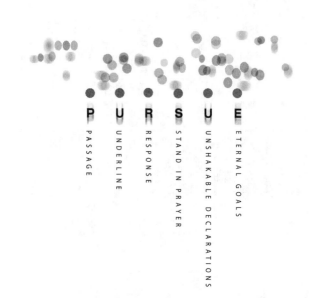

P = Passage

Take time to read through the daily passages as listed in the Bible Reading Plan in the Pursue Journal. Let the Word of God get into your heart and mind as you do your devotional reading.

U = Underline

Don't be afraid to write in your Bible. It's time to personalize it by underlining, circling and highlighting the things that really speak to you.

R = Response

Did God speak something to you through His Word today? Well, write about it already! Grab a pen and a journal and begin to write down where you are in life and what you feel God is calling you to do each day.

S = Stand in Prayer

Stand—not physically, but spiritually. After you read, pray and believe for great things in and around and through your life. Use your prayer card to help guide you as you stand in prayer.

U = Unshakable Declarations

While you're in prayer, take some time to declare the Word of God over your life. Refer to the Unshakable Declarations, and add some of your own.

E = Eternal Goals

Now what? You've read, you've underlined, you've written in your journal, you've prayed; now take the next step. As you close out your prayer and devotions, write out at least one eternal goal for today. What has God placed on your heart for your future?

As you read through each of the following chapters, you will see how you can use this simple acronym—PURSUE—to help you approach your devotions. **I hope you're ready to find all that a God-focused routine can offer.**

"REALTALK"

Jessica Neciuk
Coffee Barista

Meeting with God daily is my spiritual shot of coffee. I could not wake up without it!

Go to www.PursueGod.com to see this and other real talk quotes and interviews

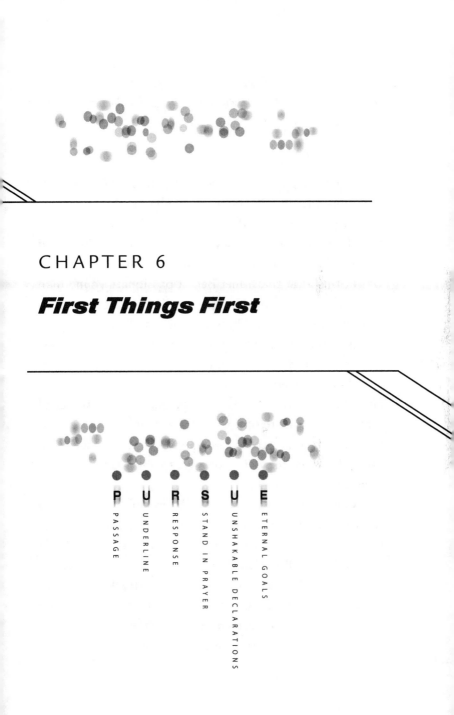

CHAPTER 6

First Things First

P U R S U E

PASSAGE

UNDERLINE

RESPONSE

STAND IN PRAYER

UNSHAKABLE DECLARATIONS

ETERNAL GOALS

Flee the evil desires of youth, and pursue righteousness, faith, love
and peace, along with those who call on the Lord out of a pure heart.
2 TIMOTHY 2:22

It was Friday night at the Generation Unleashed Conference, and more than 4,000 young people had gathered to passionately worship God. Pastor Judah Smith had just finished preaching a powerful message titled "Count the Stars," and afterward, hundreds of kids swarmed the altar for prayer. It was at this altar that I met Ben, a passionate young man who desired a complete transformation through God. Up to that point, Ben had lived a hopeless life, pursuing the things of this world. After I prayed with him, he began explaining to me his past experiences and how the GU conference had changed something inside of him. Suddenly, he encountered a real God in a real way, and it was clear that all that the world had to offer wasn't as appealing as it once had been. But the next steps weren't quite as clear. "What do I do now?" he asked me. "How do I get to know God in an authentic way?"

Many people find themselves in the same place, asking where they should start. They have a passion to pursue God that's based on their desire to have a deeper relationship with Him. But, how do they do it? **A lot of young Christians have simply been taught to pray when they eat, to take their Bible to youth group, and maybe to listen to a sermon on Sunday.** Sadly, this is the extent of their relationship with

God. If they wish, like Ben, to get to know Him in a greater, deeper way, more of their time and effort is required. It takes quantity and quality if you really want to pursue the Creator.

In answer to Ben's question, the Bible tells us in Matthew 6:33, "But, seek first his kingdom and his righteousness, and all these things will be given to you as well." How do you seek first His kingdom? The best way is through reading His Word.

"First things first . . ." I often explain to young people who are seeking answers. They sit on the edge of their seat, awaiting my response to their complex question. As I finish my statement, "read your Bible," usually they're frustrated with the simplicity of the answer. "Read your Bible," I tell them, and they stare back, waiting for more. But it's really that simple. **God's Word is His will, and His will is His Word! If you want to get closer to God, you need to read His Word on a regular basis.** As you read, you'll begin to understand how God operates. He is the same yesterday, today and forever.

According to a recent Gallup poll, about **16 percent of Americans say they read their Bible or pray on a daily basis.**[1] Such a small percentage is primarily because of these three reasons:

1. Lack of understanding
2. Lack of time
3. It's not a priority

If Christians were brutally honest with themselves, the majority would probably admit that their reason is often number three. George Barna reported that "only one out of every seven adults (15%) placed their faith in God at the top of their priority list."[2] People today simply don't give priority to the Word in their life.

I took a few minutes at the altar that night to talk with Ben and answer his "What do I do now?" question. To start, I began telling him about Stephen, whose story you can read in Acts 6–7. In my opinion, Stephen was one of the most incredible people in the New Testament. He was one of the leaders in the Early Church, a man of exceptional qualities, and I always refer to him as the first real small-group leader.

He knew how to keep "first things first." **He modeled to the messed-up culture around him what a Christian should look and act like, and he did so because of his passion for the Word of God.** He wasn't driven to be the center of attention. Rather, he strove to make God the center of attention! Regardless of the situation, he walked in faith and wisdom due to his deep relationship with God.

Stephen pursued God so fervently that those from his time claimed he was a man "full" of wisdom, faith, the Holy Spirit and grace. He wasn't living on empty, trying to make it in a world of sin. He was "full"! Everyone knew that he had a close relationship with God. There was no question that he was a believer, no wondering if he was truly a disciple of Jesus Christ. Others recognized that he walked in freedom and anointing.

What was it that made Stephen so "full"? Why did he stand out compared to those around him? The Bible shows us by Stephen's actions that there were three things that defined him and his relationship with God:

"REALTALK"

Katie Buck
Coffee Barista

Consistency and creativity have been key in making my relationship with God genuine and active. My devotions guide me in daily decisions and help me better love people. Pursue Him above all else; your days will be ordered and mercy will follow you.

Go to www.PursueGod.com to see this and other real talk quotes and interviews

1. Stephen *read* the Word of God. Read Acts 7, and you'll find that the majority of the chapter is Stephen's retelling of the Old Testament stories. Throughout the depiction of Stephen's ministry, it is clear that he had spent countless hours reading the Word. When you get the Word of God inside of your mind and heart like he did, it will change you. Stephen didn't strictly preach these stories within the four walls of a church building, and you shouldn't either! The Word of God is not meant to be exclusively a Sunday church experience. It's meant to be your best friend. As you read the Word, you will find that you are "full" of faith and have a greater desire to do God's will.

2. Stephen *retained* the Word of God. He was able to walk through the stories of the Old Testament because he had made the effort to retain them. Reading the Bible was not just a religious exercise; it was a source of wisdom, hope and faith as he locked it into memory. When you read the Word, you need to have some expectation that God will speak to you. By internalizing and retaining the Word of God, you will find that you have a well to draw from when times get tough. Pressure will always reveal what is inside of you! What are you like when the pressures of the world come crashing in?

3. Stephen *revealed* the Word of God to others. Religion without revelation is dead faith. Stephen had

a passion to share the things that God had revealed to him. We see in Acts 6 and 7 that Stephen was able to articulate the Word of God in a powerful and clear way. His ability to reveal the truth of God's Word made him stand out amongst other purely religious people. When you are "full" of the Word, it will find its way out of you.

After explaining to Ben that reading the Word of God was the first step, he got excited. I immediately saw the passion switch on in him. He wanted a deeper relationship with God, and it was evident that he was ready to do all he could to achieve that, starting with reading the Bible and getting to know God's will and His ways.

What about you? Do you still have a passion to dive into the Word daily? I would assume that you are reading this book because you, too, want to go deeper in your relationship with God and in your reading, retaining and revealing of the Word of God. You know that you desire to be "full" like Stephen. But Stephen didn't get that way through playing Xbox, surfing the Web or watching movies. First things first . . . open that Bible and discover your amazing God.

Notes
1. "Surveys Show Pastors Claim Congregants Are Deeply Committed to God, but Congregants Deny It!" The Barna Group, January 10, 2006. http://www.barna.org/barna-update/article/5-barna-update/165-surveys-show-pastors-claim-congregants-are-deeply-committed-to-god-but-congregants-deny-it?q=devotion.
2. Ibid.

What about you? Do you still have a passion to dive into the Word daily?
I would assume that you are reading this book because you, too, want to go deeper in your relationship with God and in your reading, retaining and revealing of the Word of God.

"*REALTALK*"

Elizabeth Farrell

Pursuing God is what gives me strength to get through my day. I have found there is no problem that spending time in the presence of God cannot fix.

Go to www.PursueGod.com to see this and other real talk quotes and interviews

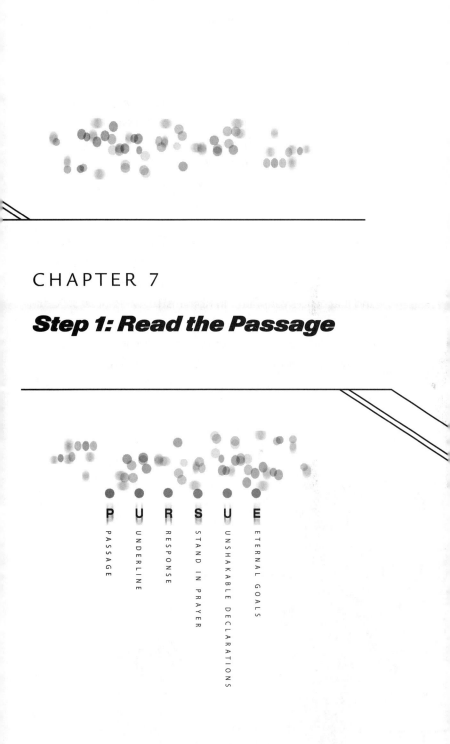

CHAPTER 7

Step 1: Read the Passage

PURSUE

P — PASSAGE

U — UNDERLINE

R — RESPONSE

S — STAND IN PRAYER

U — UNSHAKABLE DECLARATIONS

E — ETERNAL GOALS

For the word of God is living and active. Sharper than
any double-edged sword, it penetrates even to
dividing soul and spirit, joints and marrow; it judges
the thoughts and attitudes of the heart.

HEBREWS 4:12

**The first step in the "PURSUE" devotions is
"Passage."** You need to read the Word to kick off your devotions. It's the foundation of your relationship with God, and it activates your faith. In Romans 10:17, Paul says, "Consequently, faith comes from hearing the message, and the message is heard through the word of Christ."

We need more people, like Stephen, who read the Word, retain the Word and reveal it to others. The Pursue Bible read-

ing plan takes about 15 minutes a day to follow, and it takes you each year through the Old Testament once and the New Testament twice. Of course, you could read a whole lot more than this, but 15 minutes a day is a great starting point.

It may seem simple, but **God wants to speak to you through daily Bible reading.** He's just waiting for you to seek Him. Again, as God says in Jeremiah 29:13, "You will seek me and find me when you seek me with all your heart."

The Challenge

TV, movies, computer games . . . who needs reading when you have all of these? It seems like today you rarely hear young people talking about books (unless of course they involve vampires). The fact is that reading needs to become a greater part of our culture. And if the Christian youth of today really want to pursue God, they have to start by picking a passage in His Word and reading it intently!

The Bible is a hefty book, full of knowledge and understanding. Often when you approach it, it's hard to know which passage to start with. The text doesn't lay out a daily reading plan, but leaves it up to you. So, let's say you've decided to become an avid Bible reader; what's next? It's time to get practical. With the PURSUE approach to devotions, you begin with the Daily Bible Reading Plan. By doing this, you're in both the Old and the New Testament every day. It's not a binding schedule that won't allow you to skip around or read a little extra here or there. Rather, it's meant to push you toward consistency in your daily devotions.

"REALTALK"

Emma Tudorache
Small Group Leader

Spending time with God not only keeps my passion for HIM alive on a daily basis but also allows me to understand HIS real, unconditional love for the lost people I cross paths with. Prayer allows our spiritual lives to grow, and, more importantly, gives us God's perspective on what "living like Jesus" really looks like, through God's Word and His personalized message to us. It is a time we get to listen to God without interruption.

Go to www.PursueGod.com to see this and other real talk quotes and interviews

I love David's heart to daily seek God. In Psalm 63:1, he writes, **"O God, you are my God, earnestly I seek you; my soul thirsts for you, my body longs for you, in a dry and weary land where there is no water."**

As you dive into this reading plan, it's important to understand that the Bible is "living." It's not a dead book of history; it was inspired by God and is infallible! God breathed the words into being and chose men to set down His thoughts. They were moved by His Holy Spirit to record His words for us. It may be hard to wrap your head around, but imagine every page of a book being written for you. That's what God has done with His Word. He had a thousand important things He wanted you to hear, and He compiled them into one book. That's why, when you read the Word, you should expect it to speak to you.

> *All Scripture is God-breathed* and is useful for teaching, rebuking, correcting and training in righteousness, so that the man of God may be thoroughly equipped for every good work (2 Timothy 3:16-17, emphasis added).

Once you've chosen your passage and have prepared to take time and read, you need to realize that the Word of God is also active. You're not just reading another book; you're reading a book that is working something inside of you as you turn each page. If you allow it, the Word of God will directly impact you. It will penetrate even the hardest heart and speak to the very depths of the soul. It will always do something in your life in God's perfect timing!

> As the rain and the snow come down from heaven, and do not return to it without watering the earth and making it bud and flourish, so that it yields seed for the sower and bread for the eater, so is my word that goes out from my mouth: It will not return to me empty, but will accomplish what I desire and achieve the purpose for which I sent it (Isaiah 55:10-11).

It's pretty much guaranteed that the Word of God will challenge every aspect of your life. As you begin the PURSUE daily reading plan, you can be sure that God will speak to you about your attitudes. He will call on you to bring them into alignment with His Word. It may seem terrifying, but God knows exactly what you need, and He's prepared to show you.

I try to continually remind myself of the Scripture at the start of this chapter: "The Word of God is living and active. Sharper than any double-edged sword, it penetrates even to the dividing soul and spirit, joints and marrow; it judges the thoughts and attitudes of the heart" (Hebrews 4:12). **This is no ordinary book. When you read a passage from God's Word, be prepared to be challenged in your heart, spoken to through an all-powerful God and transformed to do His perfect will.**

"REALTALK"

Alicia Hayden
Junior High Pastor

My devotions aren't about finishing my
daily checklist—they're about going deeper
in relationship with Jesus. How amazing
is it that we get to be in relationship with
the creator of the universe!

Go to www.PursueGod.com to see this and other
real talk quotes and interviews

"*REALTALK*"

Jenee Fahndrich
Business Executive

I can honestly say without a shadow of a doubt that my life would have take a completely different path if I did not have a commitment to daily spending time with Jesus and His Word. No matter what trials life has thrown at me, I know that I can always look to God for strength and hope. I have come to rely completely on my daily time spent with God to live my life the way that I know I am called to live it!

Go to www.PursueGod.com to see this and other real talk quotes and interviews

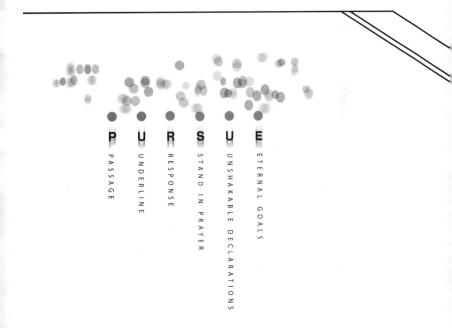

CHAPTER 8

Step 2: Underline

P U R S U E

PASSAGE

UNDERLINE

RESPONSE

STAND IN PRAYER

UNSHAKABLE DECLARATIONS

ETERNAL GOALS

"Unless you have an uncommon memory, you cannot retain the good things you hear. If you trust to your ear alone, they will escape you in a day or two; but, if you mark your Bible, and enlist the aid of your eye, you will never lose them."[1] These words of the great American evangelist Dwight L. Moody (1837–1899) are an excerpt from his sermon on Bible marking. Moody emphasized the importance of the second step in the Pursue Journal: underlining the words that speak to you in your Bible.

As Moody explained, we don't all have superhuman memory. We can't rely on ourselves to retain everything that we read or hear. That's why when we read our Bible, we should not only come to it with expectation, but also with a pen in hand.

The Bible itself challenges us to do more than just read it religiously; we need to read with anticipation of accomplishing all it says! **Anticipate that God will give you keys to living out His will and plan for your life.** James simply states it this way:

> Do not merely listen to the word, and so deceive yourselves. Do what it says. Anyone who listens to the word but does not do what it says is like a man who looks at his face in a mirror and, after looking at himself, goes away and immediately forgets what he looks like. But the man who looks intently into the perfect law that gives freedom, and continues to do this, not forgetting what he has heard, but doing it—he will be blessed in what he does (James 1:22-25).

How do we follow James's instruction and look "intently into the perfect law"? Does this mean staring hard at the Bible, hoping something gets absorbed into us? Does this mean allowing five minutes of time for a Bible verse before you run out the door, praying that God will store whatever it was you just read somewhere in your brain? The answers to these questions should be obvious. If we mean not to forget what we've just read, we need to be strategic about it. Thus, the small act of underlining is HUGELY important.

The Bible is powerful, full of wisdom and encouragement that you just might miss if you don't approach it with a practical tool like your pen. When you read it with pen in hand, you convey your anticipation and tell God that you don't simply want to be religious; you want to hear what He has to say to you. It proves you want to do more than read; you want to hear His voice and let His Word change your life. One of my heroes, Pastor Jude Fouquier of The City Church in Ventura, California, puts it this way: "A dirty Bible equals a clean mind, but a clean Bible equals a dirty mind."

The book of Joshua tells the story of a man who is leading a nation into the Promised Land. As you read his story, you learn how God performed a whole bunch of extraordinary miracles for Joshua and his people. An angel showed up and spoke to the young leader; the great walls of Jericho came crashing down as he marched the people around them; and the list goes on and on. One of the first of these amazing miracles occurred when the Jordan river at flood stage was parted so the whole nation could pass through it. When this took place, God spoke something very interesting to

"*REAL**TALK***"

Diana Dunca

The Pursue Journal has made a huge difference in my devotional life. I had a hard time choosing where to start in my Bible reading, but the Pursue Journal has helped me be more consistent in my devotions.

Go to www.PursueGod.com to see this and other real talk quotes and interviews

Joshua. He told him to get 12 stones from out of the river and set them up as a memorial on the other side. These stones signified what God had done; and in following the command God had given him, Joshua ensured that in the future, all would remember God's miraculous work.

Like these 12 stones, when you underline in your Bible, you are making a visual memorial. The goal of the underlining process is that in the future, you will remember what God spoke to you that day in your devotions. This may not be the case every time, but I have found it to be true many times in my own experience. **There are words that I underlined in my Bible 10 years ago that continue to remind me of what God has spoken to me and worked in me throughout our relationship!**

It's time for you to experience this for yourself as you read and underline in your Bible. As you do, here are three things to look for:

1. **Key words.** You should underline key words that stand out to you or that are the main thought of the passage. Key words will often help you to memorize Scripture passages. They will also help trigger God's thoughts and stir your faith when you hear them or see them again.

2. **Powerful phrases.** You should underline powerful phrases that encourage you or that have a deep sense of meaning for you. Memorizing these phrases will give you great faith when you go through hard times or need some boldness to do what God is calling you to do.

3. **Scriptures.** You should also underline Scripture verses or passages that speak to your heart and mind. Often, there are Scriptures that you will go back to time and time again as a source of encouragement or for direction.

Underlining in your Bible helps create a reference point that is easy to go back to later in life. Remember, God's Word is "living and active" (Hebrews 4:12), so He's constantly wanting to speak to you. It's time to listen; but as Dwight L. Moody put it, "don't trust to your ear alone." Take your devotional time one step further by marking the words, phrases and Scriptures that stand out to you. Now grab your pen and get ready for effective devotions.

Note
1. D. L. Moody, *Golden Counsels* (Boston, MA: United Society of Christian Endeavor, 1899). http://www.wholesomewords.org/etexts/moody/moodybmk.html.

"REALTALK"

Rick Jones
College Student

The greatest impact of the Pursue Journal is knowing that I'm diving into the same passage as my friends and small group. There's unity in that; being on the same page every day.

Go to www.PursueGod.com to see this and other real talk quotes and interviews

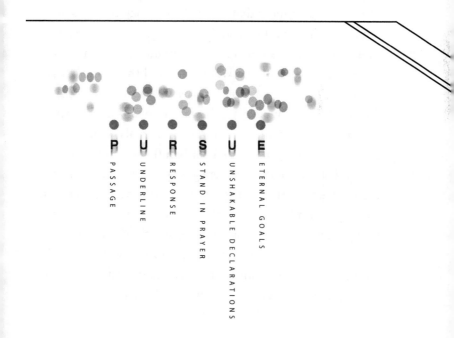

CHAPTER 9

Step 3: Write a Response

P U R S U E

PASSAGE

UNDERLINE

RESPONSE

STAND IN PRAYER

UNSHAKABLE DECLARATIONS

ETERNAL GOALS

It's Worth Remembering

Recently, I took 28 teenagers and young adults from our youth ministry to Romania on a short-term missions trip. Loading the plane with young preachers, drama teams and a talented band of musicians, I found myself bursting with excitement to find out what God had in store. As always, **God ended up exceeding all of our expectations** through powerful outreaches in the poorer areas, worship concerts where He showed up and touched countless people with His presence, and instance after instance of miraculous healings, both emotional and physical. Needless to say, it was epic!

While all of this crazy excitement was going on, I made sure that each day the team got together for devotions. We would read the Word and journal about what God was speaking to us that day. Due to the intensity of the trip, I found myself writing a lot more than normal. Every day God was doing amazing things, and I couldn't wait to get it down on paper. The entire trip was much more than any of the team could have imagined. God was working in and through each and every person. But, as it often goes with short mission trips, the "high" of those couple of weeks started to fade at the airport.

Standing there at the airport with journals filled and faith stirred, we quickly discovered our first flight was delayed two hours. This meant that we were going to miss our connecting flight back to Portland. The international traveling chaos ensued as we landed in Amsterdam and were split up into three groups, one going to Chicago, another to Minneapolis and another, my group, to Vancouver, British Columbia. In five minutes of total traveling terror, we all booked it to catch our soon-departing flights to get home. At last, we were on a plane! And . . . we stayed on that plane . . . for another long while . . . as there were mechanical difficulties (something you never want to hear from your pilot). We had been awake for 32 hours when we finally landed in Vancouver, only to find that four out of our seven bags had been lost in the insanity. So, it was one more complete night in Vancouver before we made it home to the comfort of our beds.

Sure, the journey home didn't go down quite the way I had envisioned it, but I was just happy to be home, and I knew the team would never forget all that God had accomplished on the trip. It would be impossible not to come back pumped after seeing so many people saved and healed! At least that's what I thought.

About three weeks later, my heart sank as I was talking with some of the youth in Generation Unleashed. They told me that one of their friends who went to Romania described the trip as "Okay, at best." Apparently, the flight home had ruined it for him. I was frustrated to think that someone could have had that incredible experience of God at work and remember only the bad.

The next time I saw the young man, I had to ask why he felt that way about the trip. He looked at me, shrugged and said, "It just doesn't seem like we did that much." Shocked, I replied, "How can you say that? I felt like God did lots of amazing things, and thousands of people's lives were impacted!" This didn't seem to be enough for him, so I pulled out my Pursue Journal and started listing the stuff that happened each day. My negative-attitude friend was finally convinced. "You're right, " he said, "I guess I just forgot about all that." I asked him if he had written things down like we had encouraged the whole team to do. Not surprisingly, he said, "No. I'm not really the journaling type."

We spent the next hour talking about how important it is to remember what God has done in your life. I explained to him that it's easy to forget the positive and focus on the negative. It's often our human reaction. That's why it's necessary to be intentional when it comes to reminding ourselves of God's work in our lives.

Write It Down

With the fast pace of our culture, many are realizing the need to get away from the TV and Internet and just clear their heads. Life comes at you too fast and changes so frequently that you need to make sure you have some alone time each day. Journaling is a great way to do that!

As part of your effort to pursue God, you need to take time to write a "Response" to Him and share your thoughts, both good and bad. Writing a response is a great way to really think through what God is speaking to you. But where do you start? We've already discussed underlining the things that stand out to you as you read through the Bible in your devotions. When you sit down to journal, those passages, Scriptures and words offer a perfect place for you to start in your "response." From there, you can write whatever you want to God and yourself.

> But I tell you the truth, it is to your advantage that I go away; for if I do not go away, *the Helper will not come to you;* but if I go, I will send Him to you (John 16:7, *NASB*, emphasis added).

This method to daily devotions isn't just a quick tip I came up with for this book; it's something that I have seen proven to be invaluable in my own life, time and time again. Let me give you an example: A few weeks before sitting down to write this chapter, I read John 16 in my devotions. As I read through it, verse 7 of the passage stood out to me, as well as the word "Helper." So I circled and underlined them both. After I finished my reading for the day, I opened up to one of my journal pages and wrote the word "Helper" at the top of the page. I then took the next five minutes to write out all the things I needed help with. I wrote about things related to job, family, finances, friendships that weren't the best, some project I was working on, my attitude toward specific situations currently weighing me down; and then I took some time to remind myself that the Holy Spirit is my "Helper." Because of Him, I don't have to do any of it alone.

It was amazing how my attitude and faith level completely changed after doing that simple act! Taking time to

"REALTALK"

Annalise Neciuk
Interns Pastor

As an interns pastor, it was total success taking our group through *Pursue God*. If you're looking for something to take your small group through that will bear fruit, I can't think of a better choice!

Go to www.PursueGod.com to see this and other real talk quotes and interviews

write it out helped me to refocus my mind and heart on God and His desire to walk with me through life's ups and downs. It also locked into my memory this passage from John 16, and the life principle of the Holy Spirit as my Helper. Had I just read it and moved on, I don't think that I would have had such an encounter with God.

When you take notes while a teacher or preacher is speaking, it lets that teacher know that you are there to learn, and it tends to draw more out of him/her. The act of taking out that paper and pen with keen, attentive ears makes a statement that you value what is about to be spoken. It's the same with your devotions. When you take time to write a response to what God has stirred in your heart, **you are telling God that you really value His input.** You're not going to read and forget; you are intentionally trying to lock it into memory so that it's with you the next day. James tells us that as we draw near to God, He draws near to us. Taking the time to write a response after reading God's Word is your way of showing a desire to draw closer to Him!

> Draw near to God and He will draw near to you (James 4:8, *NASB*).

So, what do you write? A lot of people find the process of journaling a daunting thing. A blank page stares back at them, and they find themselves unable to put anything into words. If you feel this way when doing your daily devotions, you may want to use these four guidelines that I find valuable when writing my "responses":

1. *Be Real with God.* Don't write a response that is some kind of religious statement that has no connection to where you actually are in life. Your written response should be a conversation with God on paper. It's you sharing your reality with your Father and best friend. That being said, however, be sure to not make your Journal just a long list of all the things you want from God. (Let's be real; selfish brats tend to drive us all crazy.) Share your heart and let Him know what you're thinking and where you are in your mind, emotions and will. If you're going to make a list of any kind, make it of issues that are on your heart, those topics and wounds that only God can understand and heal.

2. *Focus on the words you underlined.* What did God's Word speak to you as you read the passage? Often, when we write out what God spoke to us, it sinks in a lot more. If you focus on your underlined words and write them down, you will more easily remember all that God has spoken over your life. And, if you do forget, it will be there for you to return to in your Journal.

Then the LORD replied: "*Write down the revelation* and make it plain on tablets so that a herald may run with it" (Habakkuk 2:2, emphasis added).

3. *Write with expectation.* God is so amazing that He listens to us even as we write on paper! When

you take time to write out your thoughts, it can mean so much more. Even though I tell my wife I love her every day, it seems to mean a lot to her when I take the time to write it out in a note or card. When you take time to write a response to God, it means a lot to Him, showing Him that you are serious about pursuing His plan for you.

4. *Be sure to reflect on what He has done.* It's very important to never take for granted what God has done in your life. You should constantly remind yourself of all the good things He continues to accomplish for you. In order to have faith for what is in front of you, it's a good daily discipline to reflect on your past—the unique story God has created just for you.

> Look to the LORD and his strength; seek his face always. *Remember the wonders he has done,* his miracles, and the judgments he pronounced (Psalm 105:4-5, emphasis added).

I hope these four simple guidelines make the journaling process less terrifying and more exciting for you. You should be thrilled to go deeper in your relationship with God through the act of writing. Like Joshua, get ready to make "memorial stones" and never forget all the ways God comes through for you! You will find, journal entry by journal entry, that your relationship with God is growing stronger and that your faith level is growing higher.

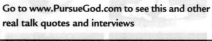

"REALTALK"

Brian Holmes
GU Intern

With the structure the Pursue Journal brings, I know what I'm reading, and it sets me up for success every morning.

Go to www.PursueGod.com to see this and other real talk quotes and interviews

CHAPTER 10

Step 4: Stand in Prayer

P PASSAGE
U UNDERLINE
R RESPONSE
S STAND IN PRAYER
U UNSHAKABLE DECLARATIONS
E ETERNAL GOALS

*What the Church needs today is not more machinery or better,
not new organizations or more and novel methods, but men whom
the Holy Ghost can use—men of prayer, men mighty in prayer.
The Holy Ghost does not flow through methods, but through men.
He does not come on machinery, but on men. He does not
anoint plans, but men, men of prayer.*

E. M. BOUNDS

In Luke 18, Jesus told His disciples another one of His many parables. With their eager attention, He began His story:

In a certain town there was a judge who neither feared God nor cared about men. And there was a widow in that town who kept coming to him with the plea, "Grant me justice against my adversary." For some time he refused. But finally he said to himself, "Even though I don't fear God or care about men, yet because this widow keeps bothering me, I will see that she gets justice, so that she won't eventually wear me out with her coming!" (verses 2-5).

When was the last time you bothered Jesus with your constant requests? That's how much Jesus wants us to pray! He wants us to pray so much that it's annoying. Weird to think of it that way, but Jesus told His disciples and all of us in this parable that we must pray continually and "wear Him out" with our pleas! Of course, it's impossible to wear Him out, but you get the point.

The fourth step in the Pursue approach asks you to do just that: Stand in Prayer. As you write out your thoughts in response to what God has spoken to you through His Word, it prepares your heart to take a stand in prayer. **This "standing" refers to a spiritual posture, not a physical stance. It's an attitude of the heart and a posture of faith.** It's important to take time each day to pray and make sure your heart is in this posture, taking a stand for the things God leads you to. In Mark 11:22-25, Jesus says:

> Have faith in God. . . . "I tell you the truth, if anyone says to this mountain, 'Go, throw yourself into the sea,' and does not doubt in his heart but believes that what he says will happen, it will be done for him. Therefore I tell you, whatever you ask for in prayer, believe that you have received it, and it will be yours. And when you stand praying, if you hold anything against anyone, forgive him, so that your Father in heaven may forgive you your sins."

Prayer Is a Big Deal

"Prayer is the most resisted activity on planet earth." I have been told this time and again by my good friend Pastor Mark Jones. Though I want to believe in the best when it comes to my fellow believers, I've found his statement rings true. Most Christians don't have a thriving prayer life. So guess what? The enemy *loves* it when we push the practice of prayer aside. He also loves it when we do it for the wrong reasons. The Bible tells us that prayer can move mountains, but it can also be a pious, religious, dead work (see Matthew 6:5-8; 17:20). Why are you praying? James tells us to check our motives at the door before we go to God in prayer (see James 1:5-6).

When the Early Church began, Luke tells us in Acts 1:14, "They all joined together constantly in prayer," revealing that prayer was their fuel. Further proving this, it later explains that it was a prayer service that actually birthed the Church. And centuries later, it is prayer that continually sustains us! Ultimately, Church history shows us that without prayer, God's Body would be like a car with no gas. We might look good, but in the end, we'd go nowhere!

Luke goes on to tell us in Acts 4:31 that "after they prayed, the place where they were meeting was shaken. And they were all filled with the Holy Spirit and spoke the word of God boldly." **As you read the Word more and more, you discover how powerful prayer can be.** In this verse, prayer was the means to a miraculous end, to a fresh touch from God and revival! Learn to pray as the Early Church prayed, and you'll find that boldness will increase in you as well!

"*REALTALK*"

Andrew Damazio
Youth Pastor

The number one thing that drastically changed my relationship with Jesus was reading my Bible and spending personal time with Jesus. The Bible is our blueprint to life. There is nothing greater to fill your mouth and heart with than God's Word.

Go to www.PursueGod.com to see this and other real talk quotes and interviews

Going Deeper in Prayer

In China, it has been said that they estimate the length of their prayers by the hour, while in America, we estimate the length of our prayers by the minute. I don't think this is most believers' intention. We want to spend time in prayer, but most people lack two things:

1. The discipline to make time in their daily schedule
2. The understanding of exactly how to pray

The first one I hope, by now, you have made a decision to fix. And if you didn't get it the first 30 times I said it, I'll say it again: Be consistent! The second one can be a little trickier. It takes time to develop an understanding of prayer, what to pray and how to pray more effectively. But if you're willing to seek after it, God will reveal it to you.

Those who are content with a lack of understanding will soon discover they have a very one-dimensional prayer life. Prayer to them is often just asking God for stuff, without truly experiencing the greater depths of His presence and power.

Even Jesus' disciples had to learn how to get beyond this one-dimensional prayer life. In Luke 11:1, the disciples came to Jesus, wanting to learn how to pray in a more passionate way. They said to Him, "Lord, teach us to pray, just as John taught his disciples." At that point in time, the disciples had been with Jesus for a while and had seen Him pray for a lot of people. They watched, we read in Luke 5, as He healed a man with leprosy; in chapter 6, we read that they watched as He restored a man's withered hand; in chapter 7, He raised a widow's son from the dead; and in chapter 8, He miraculously calmed a terrible storm and delivered someone from demons. Needless to say, the disciples had seen some things! And these are only the half of them! It was after all these astounding miracles that the disciples finally came to Jesus and asked Him to teach them to pray.

It's always interesting to me that the disciples had amazing experiences with Jesus, and yet they were not content with their current prayer lives. They had obviously prayed for people as they travelled around with Him; they had spent time watching as Jesus prayed and healed people; and still, they wanted to know more about how to pray. So, they asked Jesus how they might take their prayer to a greater level. Jesus' particular devotional time that day sparked something inside of them.

What was it about Jesus' prayer life that was so powerful? In my own study of it, I've found that there are eight fundamentals Jesus either modeled or told us to follow. And if you're going to learn from anyone, you might as well learn from the best! Take these eight points and use them as you pray. I'm confident that in making them aspects of your prayer life, you'll see Christ's power evident in your day-to-day walk like never before. I recommend using them along with the prayer card we will soon be talking about.

The Eight Prayer Fundamentals

1. Prayer is a *relationship* with God. It's through prayer that you communicate your heart to Him, while hearing the desires of His heart for you. That's why, as you continually spend time in prayer, your

ability to know and discern the will of God for your life increases.

2. Prayer is a *faith* encounter. God loves when you believe for big things, things that are only possible with His intervention. As you spend time with Him, make sure that you focus on *His* ability and not yours. As you do this, you'll discover how faith can become an active practice rather than merely a principle.

3. Prayer brings *alignment*. We need to be aware of what kind of spiritual shape we are in! If you know how to go through the motions of prayer but your personal life is out of spiritual alignment, don't expect to get too far in your time with God. God expects you to live a life that He can bless. If you get spiritually out of alignment, it affects your relationship with God. Your actions can either hinder your prayers or cause your prayers to be heard.

4. Prayer requires that you *ask*. You can never ask God too many times for something as long as you're asking with a pure heart. Remember the old widow in Jesus' parable? She asked so much that she became a bother! God wants us to ask and keep asking as a sign of trust in Him. Often people ask God for help in a situation; and if they don't get a quick response they go and try to solve it themselves. In the story about the persistent widow,

she recognizes that she can't do it on her own. She needed the judge's help; and so, she keeps asking until he gives it.

5. Prayer must have *passion*. The term "passion" refers to "a belief in something so real and valuable that it drives you to action." The Bible tells you to run the race of life with everything you have. Don't settle for a second-rate relationship with God, but passionately push and fight for one that lacks nothing.

6. Prayer requires *trust* in God's decisions. To have a vibrant devotional prayer life, you must learn to fully trust in the Lord. The word "trust" is used often in the Bible and has many meanings, among them: to have confidence, to be bold, to be secure and to be reliant on. As I read this list, the "reliance" portion sticks out most to me. What would it look like if we were all truly reliant on our God? In a highly individualistic society, this concept can be a hard one to grasp. But if we learn to lean on Him and trust Him for things to come, we'll encounter blessing, grace and growth like never before!

7. Prayer is *motivated by love*. When love becomes your motivation for prayer, you'll find you're no longer simply focused on yourself. It's so easy to make prayer all about your problems, desires and needs. But when you allow love to take over, it causes you

to put God's will and others' needs first, rather than your own. When you let love drive your prayers, it makes for a longer, more meaningful time with God, rather than a quick, shallow meet-and-greet.

8. Prayer is *purpose driven*. Do you know why you pray? It's not simply so that you can practice being religious. It's so that you can get to know God and His specific will for your life. As you take time to pray with a purpose, you will soon find that you are hearing God's voice. Daily praying tells God that you value His opinions and you want Him to lead and guide you through this life.

As you can see, there are many aspects of prayer to think about. But don't let them bog you down. The act of prayer is really very simple. You're just talking with God, opening up your mouth and chatting it up with your Father, your Best Friend, the Big Guy who created you. Okay . . . well, maybe at the start it can be a little overwhelming. He's so great and we are so, well, *not*. What's amazing is that He, who created the swirling, epic galaxies above us, *wants* to talk to you and me and wants to hear from us.

The Pursue Prayer Card

I've come up with three simple boxes in one little prayer card to make the practice easy. The goal is to help you in developing a powerful prayer life by keeping it simple. If you have a Pursue Journal, go to page 17, find the Pursue prayer card and take some time to fill it out. This card contains three boxes: (1) people, (2) things and (3) goals. If you don't have a Pursue Journal, I recommend that you get one or make a similar page in whatever you use to record your life and times.

In the first box, make a list of all the people you would like to pray for. This could be pastors, family, friends, co-workers, political leaders, people you know are experiencing hard times, or people you have a rough relationship with. In the second box, start listing all the "things" you need and want to pray for (your work environment, our nation, the school you go to, your finances, politics, your church, campus club, your relationships, and so on). This list will grow as you take time to pray it through. In the third box, write "Goals." List all the goals you have. These could be anything from sharing your faith more to saving money or quitting an addiction. The list is meant to work as a starting place, a first step toward a greater prayer life. As you pray more frequently, you'll find that the Holy Spirit will speak to you about more people, things and goals for your list.

I know that you might hold this list in your hand and simply check the boxes. But that's not its intention. The prayer card is meant to work as a reference guide to help you go deeper in prayer. If you take the time to pray for people, you'll find that the Holy Spirit will place specific things on your heart regarding them, such as Scriptures to declare over their lives. Soon you'll find that you'll only need to glance at your prayer card a few times as you spend time with God interceding for others, for the things you've written down and for your specific goals.

Standing in Prayer for . . .

Colossians 4:2

Devote yourselves to prayer, being watchful and thankful.

✳ People

✳ Things

✳ Goals

Sample taken from page 17 of the Pursue Journal

"REALTALK"

Cassie Davis

Here's something: Colossians 3:16 says, "Let the Word of God dwell in you richly." For me, the more I get the Word, the richer my life gets. Simple as that.

Go to www.PursueGod.com to see this and other real talk quotes and interviews

Write Down the Answered Prayers

I like to keep a page to record the prayers that God has answered. I know what you're thinking: "I won't forget what He's done!" Well, you'd be surprised how often God answers prayers and we just let them drift away from our memory. That's why you have to write it down! I often look at this page of my Pursue Journal to remind myself how powerful prayer is. God listens and answers as we do our part to make our requests known.

I'd like to conclude this chapter with a challenge. It's time to find a friend to hold you accountable to daily prayer. Proverbs 27:17 states, **"As iron sharpens iron, so one man sharpens another." Life was never meant to be lived alone. That's why you have relationships with others.** They are there to help you stand strong. This is especially the case in the family of God. You need to latch on to someone who can help and encourage you to set aside time for God. Often, the littlest encouragement can go the longest way.

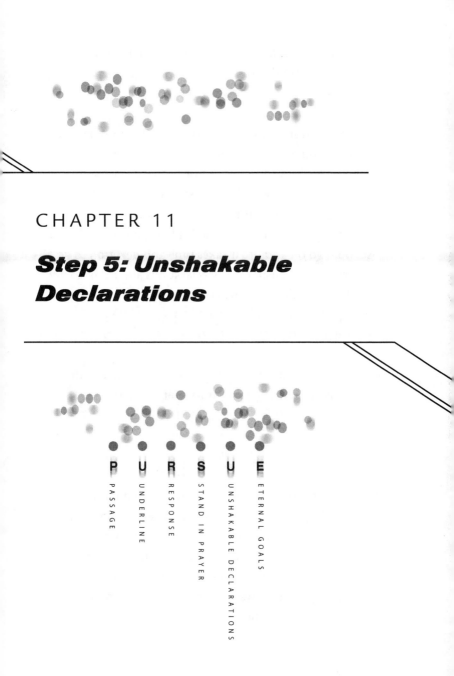

CHAPTER 11

Step 5: Unshakable Declarations

PURSUE

PASSAGE
UNDERLINE
RESPONSE
STAND IN PRAYER
UNSHAKABLE DECLARATIONS
ETERNAL GOALS

> *For the king trusts in the LORD; through the unfailing*
> *love of the Most High he will not be shaken.*
>
> PSALM 21:7

As this psalm states, with God on our side, nothing can rattle us. It's time to declare statements like these—the truths of the Bible—as facts over our lives! That's why the fifth step in the PURSUE approach is "Unshakable Declarations."

Have you ever wanted to take something to the next level? Maybe your grades, athletic ability, musical talent, the list could go on and on. It takes time and devotion to go beyond the norm. Unshakable Declarations are meant to boost your Bible-reading and prayer time to become more than the average devotions. **Put faith in God's Word over your life and watch as you grow deeper in Him.**

Death and life are in the power of the tongue, and those who love it will eat its fruit (Proverbs 18:21, *NASB*).

The Next Level

When I first started praying, I always felt that if I wasn't literally shouting at the devil for an hour, I hadn't stirred my faith up enough. I rarely felt like I went deep enough in prayer, and I was constantly disappointed in myself. I also continually questioned my motives. Why was I praying? Was it enough for God? I genuinely wanted to pray with more faith, but I couldn't really grasp how to go about it.

Then, I got a revelation of how powerful God's Word is. The Word of God is living and active! It dawned on me that if I wanted my prayer life to go to another level, I needed to begin to incorporate the Word of God into it. Sounds simple and obvious, but for me, it was one of those "light bulb goes on" moments.

As I grew in my understanding of the relationship between prayer and God's Word, I began to combine them in my devotions. Reading the Word and leaving it at that wasn't enough anymore. I started actually praying it! **This radically changed my prayer life. Immediately, my faith grew, and my expectation no longer wavered, because I stopped simply praying my will and started praying God's!**

> Consequently, faith comes from hearing the message, and the message is heard through the word of Christ (Romans 10:17).

If you really want to go to the next level in your prayer times, you can't rely on yourself. The Word of God is infallible, absolute and powerful. Allow it to take you higher.

This is why the fifth step in the PURSUE devotional plan is Unshakable Declarations. This step is a means to help you go deeper in prayer through the Word, while stirring your faith for supernatural results. As you begin to declare the Declarations (written on the following pages) over your life—declarations about your family, friends, goals and the things on your prayer card—you will go deeper in prayer. You can even start memorizing some of the Unshakable Declarations and use them throughout your day. When we declare God's Word over our lives, our doubt regarding our own capabilities, and God's, begins to fade and our faith begins to grow.

Jesus Did It, So Why Don't We?

Being a man, Jesus endured temptation just as we do, and the Bible gives us opportunity to see how He handled it (see Matthew 4:1-11).

Jesus had just fasted for 40 days when He faced His greatest temptation, in the wilderness. There He was, starving, and there the devil was, asking Him to turn a rock into bread. Sure, He could have done it. He could have made a whole feast if He wanted! But rather than giving in to the devil's plot, He turned to the Word, and those simple declarations freed Him from the enemy's grasp. He conquered temptation with simple quotations spoken aloud!

This story reveals the true purpose of the Word of God. It's meant to act as a weapon. Four times the devil tried to tempt Jesus, and every time He used this greatest of weapons to thwart His adversary. In doing so, He gave us a clear example of how to defeat the enemy's schemes in our own lives.

But the Word doesn't stop there. It's not simply designed to act as your Sword, but also as your Light. When we declare the Word of God in our prayer time, we are saying that we trust in His direction for our life. Therefore, a declaration becomes an act of humility and surrender to God's guidance and light.

Your word is a lamp to my feet and a light for my path (Psalm 119:105).

Now that we understand these two key purposes of the Bible and how Unshakable Declarations play a part in them, it's time to start doing something about it. On the following pages I've listed 10 of my favorite Unshakable Declarations. These are just to start you off and get you confident in speaking faith over your life. Don't limit yourself to just these declarations. Instead, make a habit of writing down any verses that you feel work as Unshakable Declarations for you. Write them in your Pursue Journal and speak them over your life every day!

Ten Unshakable Declarations

1. I Am Called to Preach the Gospel!

"Go into all the world and preach the Good News to everyone" (Mark 16:15, *NLT*). Declare that today you're called to preach the living gospel of Jesus Christ. No matter your gender, age, status or spiritual anointing, *everyone* is called to preach.

2. I Am a New Creation in Christ!

"Therefore, if anyone is in Christ, he is a new creation; the old has gone, the new has come!" (2 Corinthians 5:17). Declare that you are a new creation in Christ, and you don't have to let the past plague your heart and mind anymore. New, unimaginably amazing things will come your way today!

3. I Have a Great Future!

"'For I know the plans I have for you,' declares the LORD, 'plans to prosper you and not to harm you, plans to give you hope and a future'" (Jeremiah 29:11). Declare that God has great things in store for you! You are not destined for a small, worthless future. God has epic plans for your life—better than anything you could come up with on your own.

4. I Can Do All Things Through Christ Who Strengthens Me!

"I can do everything through him who gives me strength" (Philippians 4:13). Declare that God has equipped you with all you need to fulfill His will for today. Don't bow down to insecurity and fear; go after everything God has placed in your heart!

5. By His Stripes I Am Healed!

"But he was wounded and crushed for our sins. He was beaten that we might have peace. He was whipped, and we were healed!" (Isaiah 53:5, *NLT*). Declare that God will enact His supernatural touch in and through your life. Pray for those who need God's healing power—naturally, spiritually and emotionally.

6. No Weapon Formed Against Me Shall Prosper!

"No weapon that is formed against you will prosper" (Isaiah 54:17, *NASB*). Declare to the enemy that he will not have his way over your life! Ask God to build a hedge of protection around your heart and mind, and the path you walk today.

7. I Will Not Give In to Temptation!

"But remember that the temptations that come into your life are no different from what others experience. And God is faithful. He will keep the temptation from becoming so strong that you can't stand up against it. When you are tempted, he will show you a way out so that you will not give in to it" (1 Corinthians 10:13, *NLT*). Declare that today will be a day of victory over the devil's plan in your life! Pray that God would make clear to you the way out of the temptations that trip you up each day.

8. God Will Speak to Me Today as I Pray!

"Call to me and I will answer you and tell you great and unsearchable things you do not know" (Jeremiah 33:3). Declare that God's voice will be alive and active in your life! You're not just speaking to the wind. Therefore, it's time to expect to hear what your Creator wants to say to you each day.

9. I Am Free in Christ!

"It is for freedom that Christ has set us free. Stand firm, then, and do not let yourselves be burdened again by a yoke of slavery" (Galatians 5:1). Declare the freedom you have in Christ! You are not bound to the old ways and old habits of yesterday. You are free! Pray for 100 percent freedom in areas in which you are still feeling even the slightest bit bound.

10. I Am Pure in Christ!

"If we confess our sins, he is faithful and just and will forgive us our sins and purify us from all unrighteousness" (1 John 1:9). Declare that your purity is found in Christ! Don't let past struggles define your future. Walk in the purity that the cross has provided you.

As you incorporate the Unshakable Declarations into your prayer life, you'll find new grace and strength to overcome the challenges of each day. Your Unshakable Declarations from God's Word help you battle the enemy and your own insecurities. Remember, even Jesus didn't try to overcome the enemy with His overwhelming wit and strength. He simply stated the Word of God with confidence. You can too. **When you pray God's Word, you can be sure you are praying His will!**

How can a young man keep his way pure?
By living according to your word.
I seek you with all my heart;
do not let me stray from your commands.
I have hidden your word in my heart
that I might not sin against you.
Praise be to you, O LORD;
teach me your decrees.
With my lips I recount
all the laws that come from your mouth.
I rejoice in following your statutes
as one rejoices in great riches.
I meditate on your precepts
and consider your ways.
I delight in your decrees;
I will not neglect your word.

PSALM 119:9-16

"*REALTALK*"

Danielle Bentley

It's not the many hours of prayer that the Lord seeks from us, it's the amount of heart put into those prayers that He desires most!

Go to www.PursueGod.com to see this and other real talk quotes and interviews

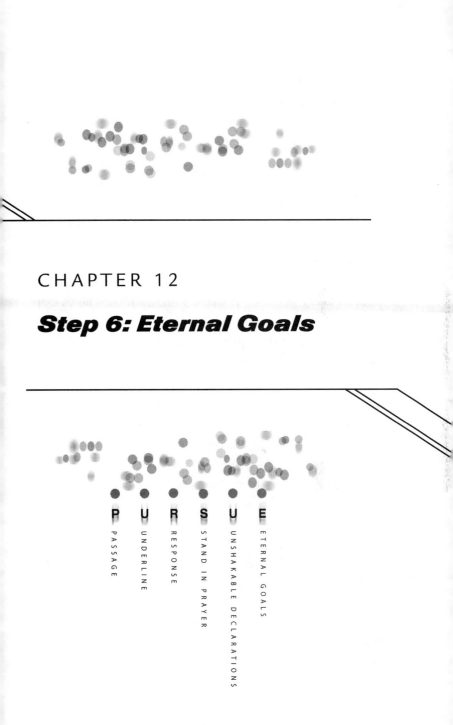

CHAPTER 12

Step 6: Eternal Goals

P PASSAGE

U UNDERLINE

R RESPONSE

S STAND IN PRAYER

U UNSHAKABLE DECLARATIONS

E ETERNAL GOALS

Alas, we have finally reached the last step in the PURSUE approach to your devotions. I like to call this the "Now What?" portion. You've read, you've underlined, you've written in your journal, you've prayed; now take the next step. As you close out your prayer and devotions, write out at least one eternal goal for today. What has God placed on your heart for this moment in your life?

What are you going to live for? Often, we live on autopilot, thinking we'll have years upon years to fulfill all that is in our hearts to accomplish. But the reality is that we don't know what tomorrow holds. That's why everyone has to daily answer this question, make this choice and know what he or she is living for. It just may be that today is the last chance you have to impact someone's life. Have you seriously thought about it that way?

> One thing, and only one, in this world has eternity stamped upon it. Feelings pass; resolves and thoughts pass; opinions change. What you have done lasts—lasts in you. Through ages, through eternity, what you have done for Christ, that, and only that, you are. (Frederick W. Robertson, 1816–1853)

I like how James puts it: "Come now, you who say, today or tomorrow we will go into such and such a city and spend a year there and carry on our business and make money. Yet you do not know [the least thing] about what may happen tomorrow. What is the nature of your life? You are [really] but a wisp of vapor (a puff of smoke, a mist) that is visible for a little while and then disappears [into thin air]. You

ought instead to say, if the Lord is willing, we shall live and we shall do this or that [thing]" (James 4:13-15, *AMP*).

James urges that we, as Christians, **don't put off God's will until tomorrow. God desires it for us today!** That's why it's so important to end your devotions each day with contemplating, setting goals and beginning to walk in the eternal plan for your life.

When I was 16, I learned what a vapor life could really be. It was summertime. I had tons of friends; I was a leader in my youth group; and life was all around pretty good. I remember feeling like I was really tracking strong with God on a personal note, keeping away from all the "bad stuff" that the worldly people did. I thought I had it all together, but I realize now that I was very self-focused. Each day was about me, and what I wanted.

Then came the wake-up call. It started on a Friday night while I was on my way to youth group. I picked up two of my friends and, like always, we showed up looking to have a good time. There were a lot of new people there that night. I remember walking in and immediately being taken by surprise at the sight of one of these newbies. His name was Kenny, and I knew him from school. Kenny wasn't exactly the best kid—a little rough around the edges—and it felt strange to see him at church. I gave him a short "Hi" and a head-nod and went to my seat. That was the extent of our interaction.

Worship and the Word that night were both really powerful, and lots of young people were touched. Then it came time for the altar call. The pastor asked us all to bow our heads and close our eyes. "Is there anyone here who wants to get their life right with Jesus, and ask Him to forgive your sins?" he said into the mic. Unable to help myself, I peeked and saw a few hands pop up. I scanned the room and landed on the person who interested me most. Would tonight be Kenny's night? I noticed him fidgeting a little in his seat. Maybe he was going to raise his hand? But the altar call came and went, and Kenny stayed where he was.

Later that night, I had a second chance to talk with him. I could have walked right up and said more than hello. Distracted by the fun I was having just hanging with my friends, I didn't approach Kenny. I decided against stepping out of the old comfort zone.

Saturday came, and it was back to my usual routine. I slept in, read my Bible, said a quick prayer and went about my day. For some reason, I couldn't get Kenny off my mind, but I didn't do anything about it.

The next day, I got dressed in my Sunday finest and went to church. It seemed like any other Sunday, and I was excited to be at one of my favorite places. I remember distinctly walking through the doors, thinking all was well, when one of my friends ran up to me and immediately asked if I had heard about what happened to Kenny the night before. Obviously, I had no clue. Kenny and I weren't close. I had a chance to talk to him but had let it slip by. I didn't know much about his day-to-day activities. I wasn't prepared for the next bit of information. My friend proceeded to tell me how Kenny had left a party in a car with a drunk driver. On the way home, they got in a horrible wreck. Kenny had died. I stood there in shock.

I know that in moments like these we're often told, "Don't beat yourselves up about it. There's nothing you could have done. It's not your fault this happened." I don't know about all of that, but I do know this: I had a chance to impact someone's life in eternity, and because I was too absorbed in my own happiness, I failed to do anything about it. The Holy Spirit had been nudging me to reach out to Kenny, and in response, what had I done? I hung out with my friends; I stayed in my bubble. I didn't even pray for him during my devotions. What if I had just talked to him? What if I had been a little bit more eternally focused that Friday night, or in my devotions on Saturday? Maybe things would have been different.

Every day, we are surrounded by "Kennys"—people who need to encounter a loving God, and who are seeking truth but don't know where to look. First Timothy tells us that it's God's will and desire that all people would be saved. He wants to use you and me to reach all people with His love and grace. But will we take our eyes off all the temporal things around us and start to focus on the eternal?

> This is good, and pleases God our Savior, who wants all men to be saved and to come to a knowledge of the truth (1 Timothy 2:3-4).

The great evangelist and missionary to China Hudson Taylor (1832–1905) said this:

> Perhaps if there were more of that intense distress for souls that leads to tears, we should more frequently see the results we desire. Sometimes it may be that while we are complaining of the hardness of the hearts of those we are seeking to benefit, the hardness of our own hearts and our feeble appre-

"REALTALK"

Keirsten Jones
High School Pastor

Ever since I've been using my Pursue Journal, my prayer life has gone to a whole new level. Before, I was missing the depth of true intercession. I love that the Pursue Journal reminds me to continually be praying for specific people, specific miracles and mountains that need to be moved!

Go to www.PursueGod.com to see this and other real talk quotes and interviews

hension of the solemn reality of eternal things may be the true cause of our want of success.

If there's one thing I definitely learned from my experience that summer I was 16, when a high-school acquaintance died, it's that we need to live life on purpose, never taking for granted the opportunity to impact someone's life. **You need to have an eternal perspective as you spend time with God each day. Prayer is not just about your needs; it's also about preparing you for the day ahead.** During your prayer time, God will often give you insight for your day and a stirring in your heart for someone He wants you to pay attention to or something He wants you to do.

What is one goal that God would have you focus on today? Each day you should ask God to help you identify an eternal goal for that day—something you can do that will make a difference in eternity. Here are some simple eternal goals that I often focus on. Feel free to use some of them, or ask the Holy Spirit to make others clear to you.

Eternal Goals

1. I Will Share My Faith with Someone Today

Once you begin to share your faith, you'll find that it's not as hard as you thought. In Romans 10:14-15, Paul says, "How, then, can they call on the one they have not believed in? And how can they believe in the one of whom they have not heard? And how can they hear without someone preaching to them? And how can they preach unless they are sent? As it is written, 'How beautiful are the feet of those who bring good news!'" There are so many people around you that need to hear about the love of God and that He has a plan and purpose for them. It's time to start praying for an opportunity to share your faith with someone!

2. I Will Meet Someone's Need Today

Take time to meet someone else's need before your own. You might just find that life gets a little better. In Mark 12:29-31, Jesus says, "The most important [commandment] . . . is this . . . 'Love the Lord your God with all your heart and with all your soul and with all your mind and with all your strength.' The second is this: 'Love your neighbor as yourself.' There is no commandment greater than these." Be a conduit of His love to the people around you today.

3. I Will Draw Near to God Throughout My Day

James 4:8 says, "Draw near to God and He will draw near to you" (NASB). Make it your goal to continue to pursue God throughout your day. This should be an intentional practice, not something you simply hope happens naturally.

4. I Will Build Up Someone Today

Paul says in 1 Thessalonians 5:11, "Therefore encourage one another and build each other up, just as in fact you are doing." Today, make it a goal to build someone up. In your prayer time, ask God if there is someone He wants you to encourage or bless.

5. I Will Live Life Focused on God's Purposes

In 2 Thessalonians 1:11, Paul says, "We constantly pray for you, that our God may count you worthy of his calling, and that by his power he may fulfill every good purpose of yours and every act prompted by your faith." Don't just go through the motions each day; be intentional in all that you do.

Make Every Day Count

Ever since I began approaching my devotions this way, with expectation and with focus on my life's eternal impact, God has not failed to open my eyes to daily opportunities. I'm excited to tell you that because I have become more concerned with eternity than my own happiness, I've seen many people like Kenny make decisions for Christ.

As you wrap up prayer during your devotions each day, **ask God to reveal to you one thing you should be focusing on.** Make sure you're truly open to the Holy Spirit speaking to you about the people who surround you and the countless opportunities you have to impact these people's lives each day. Do this and watch as God transforms the significance of your life. It's a beautiful feeling to look back on your day and recognize that you made a dent in the grand scope of eternity.

Be joyful always; pray continually; give thanks in all circumstances, for this is God's will for you in Christ Jesus.
1 THESSALONIANS 5:16-18

It's a beautiful feeling to look back on

your day and recognize that you made a dent

in the grand scope of eternity.

"REALTALK"

Andrea Jones
College Student

The Pursue Journal has really helped me
to stay on track with my devotions. It's
important to actually be talking with God
and reading His Word on a daily basis.

Go to www.PursueGod.com to see this and other
real talk quotes and interviews

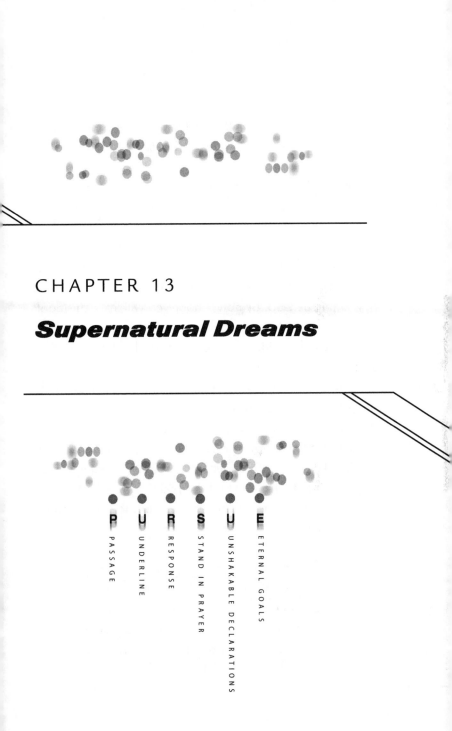

CHAPTER 13

Supernatural Dreams

P PASSAGE

U UNDERLINE

R RESPONSE

S STAND IN PRAYER

U UNSHAKABLE DECLARATIONS

E ETERNAL GOALS

Supernatural Dreams are the result of knowing you are loved by God for who you are, not for what you do.

When God's "super" meets our "natural," anything is possible!
PASTOR JACK LOUMAN, CITY BIBLE CHURCH

Here we are, at the close of this journey we've traveled together. I've written about the *why* you pursue God and the *how* to pursue God. By now, I hope you will leave this book challenged to take your devotions to the next level. It only seems fitting to finish where we started, where everyone started, in the Garden.

The goal of this book is not to get a bunch of young people pumped for a couple of short weeks. I didn't want to merely "fire you up," as we youth pastors too often say. Rather, I started writing with a dream that a generation would, like never before, become inspired and equipped to step out of hiding and PURSUE a real God who loves them, forgives them and wants the very best for them. Now about that Garden . . .

> In the last days, God says, I will pour out my Spirit on all people. Your sons and daughters will prophesy, your young men will see visions, your old men will dream dreams. Even on my servants, both men and women, I will pour out my Spirit in those days, and they will prophesy (Acts 2:17-18).

In chapter 1, we looked at how Adam and Eve were lost in the very place God had called them to be. They had a direct contact with their Creator, a relationship with Him, and yet, because of sin, they went into hiding. Don't let the enemy convince you that you need to hide yourself from God like they did.

It's time for a little honesty. Look at your life and answer these questions: **Where are you in your journey with God? Do you really believe that God has something supernatural in store for you? Do you think that God loves you for who you are . . . or do you still think your works make you unworthy?**

God loved you before you ever did anything right or wrong. Grab hold of the reality of the depth of His love for you. And while you're doing that, you might as well begin to dream some supernatural dreams! I'm talking out-of-the-box stuff. God doesn't fit into your perfect plan or even the scope of your wildest imagination. I want you to leave this book fixing your eyes on *His* ability, not yours.

Be a Joseph in Your Generation

I firmly believe that this is a Joseph generation, and that as you spend time pursuing God each day, you'll find that God will open doors for you like He did for Joseph. We've already discussed the compass mentality that God placed in Joseph (he didn't have a map for his life, but he always had that compass with north pointing toward his faith in God). Now I want to dive into his story again and discuss his ability to dream. Joseph dared to believe in the dream God had given him. At the age of only 17, he felt that God, through the many visions and dreams God gave him, was nudging him toward greatness. The exact details of this greatness weren't clear, but he knew that somehow God would put him in a place of influence.

God had instilled this supernatural dream in Joseph, and though he was scoffed at and thrown into a pit by his brothers, he refused to let go of the dream. Even in the deepest, darkest pit, Joseph held on to the purposes of God for his life.

So often people today let go of their dream when they encounter hardship. Joseph quickly turned his dark loneliness into alone time with God. He stayed the course, and we know he fulfilled the purposes of God for his life and his generation.

God's Affirmation, Not the World's Confirmation!

If you want to be like Joseph and pursue the "Supernatural Dream" God has for you, then you need to long for God's affirmation, not the world's confirmation. As you spend time in the Word each day, let it reiterate what God is calling you to do. Don't look to the things of this world to dictate your direction and ability in life. Where you are today is only the starting point of your destiny. In just one moment, God could raise you to places you never thought imaginable!

What's always incredible to me about Joseph's story is that in just a matter of hours, he went from being a prisoner to being Pharaoh's right-hand man. It was all in the plan and purpose of God to save an entire nation and continue His promises to His chosen people. It's not your job to make sure the dream happens; God will take care of that. All you have to do is be faithful, regardless of what the journey throws at you.

Never forget that dreams like Joseph's and your own often are accompanied by seasons of loneliness, which is a familiar territory for all of us. I have already talked about this generation's reliance on technology. Today, we are both more connected and lonelier than ever before. Follow Joseph's example and turn those feelings of isolation into moments of alone time with God. Without tests and trials, there would be no testimony declaring God's faithfulness. Pursue the dream God has placed on your heart, no matter what trials come your way.

So what are you going to do now that you know that you are called to live life on purpose? Will you be a Joseph in your generation?

Now to him who is able to do immeasurably more than all we ask or imagine, according to his power that is at work within us, to him be glory in the church and in Christ Jesus throughout all generations, for ever and ever! Amen (Ephesians 3:20-21).

Will you pursue the dream God puts in your heart, making the most of every moment in life and focusing on God's will? Or will you be like Adam and Eve, hiding from God because of your weakness? Choose to have *eternal significance* rather than *temporal success*. This comes with knowing God personally and making His love and grace known to all those around you.

It's time! Now that you have an understanding of the PUR-SUE approach, take it for a test drive. **Commit to getting to know God more on a daily basis, to watching as you grow deeper, to dreaming bigger and to hearing His voice like never before. Then watch how it affects the world around you when a new desire to share your faith and see God's epic will accomplished takes over!** The tools are in your hands; the dreams and their eternal significance are stretched out in front of you. What are you waiting for?

Begin the beautiful pursuit of God today.

Begin the beautiful **pursuit of God** today.

The Attitude of Faith
By Pastor Frank Damazio

The "yes" attitude is the biblical attitude for living life. God's Word is faithful, and His message is absolute, certain and guaranteed. God does not vacillate in His message or His plans, and neither should we. More than just positive thinking or mind over matter, author Frank Damazio describes an attitude established upon the Word of God. More than fantasizing or imagining whatever we want, it is saying yes to the God who can and will do exceedingly and abundantly above all that we ask or think. For more resources from Pastor Frank Damazio, go to www.FrankDamazio.com.

What Now
By Pastor Marc Estes

God's intent is that we live life purposefully and deliberately, not randomly. Each of us has been given a measure of passions, gifts, talents and abilities to invest during our lifetime. How we use or misuse them creates consequences. Ultimately, each of us will be held responsible for what we were given and whether we were faithful in making our lives count. *What Now* will help you to make sense of who you are and where you are going! What makes this book unique are seven distinct self-discovery tests that will specifically define key areas of your life. This is a must-read. For more resources from Pastor Marc Estes, go to www.MarcEstes.com.

Generation Unleashed® // Saving Power CD/DVD
The Generation Unleashed band firmly believes that the presence of God changes people's lives. This CD captures this generation's passion and desire to see God lifted high with songs that create a culture of presence-driven worship. The Generation Unleashed band takes God's message of hope and freedom in Jesus Christ to churches, conferences, cities and nations worldwide. To find out more, go to www.Facebook.com/GenerationUnleashed.

Portland Bible College

For more than 40 years, the passion of Portland Bible College has been to partner with the Church to develop leaders in all areas of life that will influence, impact and transform their world. Portland Bible College offers training in pastoral leadership, worship and creative arts, pastoral counseling and youth ministry, along with a humanities program designed for university transfer. At Portland Bible College, you'll find a vibrant campus where you will experience God's presence, clearly understand His Word, walk with a team of staff and pastors committed to your success, and be equipped to fulfill God's vision for your life! For more information, go to www.PortlandBibleCollege.com.

"*REALTALK*"

Poncho Lowder
Inspiring people to pursue God is the passion of my life! (@PastorPoncho)

Pastor Poncho Lowder speaks both nationally and internationally, with a focus on equipping and empowering people in their pursuit of God. For booking, email Poncho@CityBibleChurch.org. You can connect with Poncho on Facebook at www.Facebook.com/PastorPoncho. Also listen to his weekly podcast on iTunes.